MW01611227

IDENTITY

Peter J. Wamono

1

Identity.
Copyright © 2021. Peter J. Wamono.

ISBN: 978-163821268-3

Printed in the United States of America.

Table of Contents

Preface

This book is a true story of how a young man born in poverty, alcoholism and dysfunction in Uganda, East Africa, found God or was found by God and experienced transformation that brought about a 180-degree turn in his life. This was a u-turn that has affected and continues to affect his family and the community and city where he was born. I have had the privilege of traveling to much of the world over the last 18 years and I do not say that lightly because growing up, even getting to the airport just to see a plane take off was winning in life for me. But, I could not even manage that.

I have learned over the years walking with Jesus that true poverty is not just the absence of material blessing, but the absence of the true love of God in life. Growing up, we lacked material blessings, but we also lacked God. Don't get me wrong now; we went to church every Sunday. My late mother made sure we did. We always had religion. There is a difference between having religion and having God in your life.

This book is about how I found God, how God found me, how that affected the trajectory of my life and continues to

shape the man I am continually becoming. It is an honest story about the depth of depravity God called me out of, my brokenness, my weaknesses and failures, doubts, shortcomings, fears, losses, gains, successes and adventures. This book is a true tale of a life touched, revealed, exposed and transformed by the living God. I have been as honest as I can possibly be about things I worked so hard to hide about myself for a long time in order to keep up appearances. This book is a reveal of my journey to discovering God and unveiling me and my purpose, and I think it can help someone looking for their own meaning and purpose in life. It is not deep theology, just a true story of a life transformed. I think many people may find themselves somewhere in these pages at one point in their lives. I pray and hope in reading this that the reader will find the true freedom in Jesus that I have found and keep finding as I daily become the man God created me to be. The journey to your dreams and your purposes in this world is the journey to discovering yourself and discovering the one true God.

Introduction

I will proclaim the Lord's decree. He said to me, "You are my son. Today, I have become your father. Ask me, and I will make the nations your inheritance, the ends of the earth your possession."

(Psalms 2:7-8)

This portion of scripture describes well what I have come to discover the extent of my calling in life entails. I was born in Eastern Uganda in a town called Mbale. Both my parents were teachers. We were very poor. In Uganda, when you are poor, even the government cannot help you. You are on your own. I grew up wearing air-conditioned clothes. If you don't know what these are, they were raggedy old clothes with holes in them. When you ran, the wind blew right through you. It was a cool feeling, actually. People wear these kinds of jeans as a fashion trend these days and pay a lot for them too. I would like to put it on record that my siblings and I started this fashion trend a long time ago. We were trend setters without knowing it. Thinking

of this, I should have patented my childhood swag. We would be laughing all the way to the bank now, hahaha.

I walked 4 miles to school from the age of 5, much of that barefoot. We measured the temperature of the hot, sunbaked dirt paths with the soles of our feet, often shuffling our dirt-covered feet between the dirt and old pothole-filled bitumen road surface that had seen better days when Uganda was still a colony under British authority.

We were poor, but we had fun as kids growing up. With an alcoholic father and a mother struggling to make ends meet, we often had no restrictions. We were like free-range kids looking back now. Do not get me wrong, my mother was a tough disciplinarian. The rod was always applied when was required, but we had freedom to roam. When you do not have much, you have to be creative.

We climbed big rocks, went mango hunting, beat the ground with sticks where ants had built a mound so edible ants would come out and we could have an ant-eating feast in our air-conditioned swag. This is actually true! We made our own toys. We made guns out of sticks and pretended to shoot at each other. We knew about guns because I grew up in the era Uganda was starting to recover from the turbulence of war. I was born December 1979, the same year Idi Amin who had subjected the nation to a brutal dictatorship was deposed and kicked out of Uganda. Like I often say, he knew I was coming. I made my first toy car before my 7th birthday. It was made of copper wires and held together by strips of black rubber band. I called my first toy car a Honda.

My father was an alcoholic who drunk himself lame and often had to be carried home from the bar. Because of my father's drinking habits, my parents always had fights and threw all kinds of demeaning words at each other. It got physical sometimes. I was not proud of my parents growing up. I loved my mother, was always on her side, but was very embarrassed about my father. My siblings and I often wished we were part of a different family or that we did not have an earthly father. We thought it better to have been orphans than to have a father that the community ridiculed our family for. We were often mocked and written off by some as not good enough and will never amount to much courtesy of our dad's alcoholism. This was my inheritance, folks! But God had different plans. He saw us then as He sees us now. God sees you. He knows you, no matter where you are and how you feel right now about yourself.

My mother tried her best to get us into the best schools possible, even with limited or no resources. Like I said, we walked a long distance to and from school from a young age, and this was because our mother wanted us to be in the best primary school in our town - Rock View Primary School in Tororo, Eastern Uganda, the place we spent our formative years.

I was a very unstable child. I did not have an identity. I wanted to be anyone but who I really was. I remember the time I stole pair of shoes I had seen hanging off a dormitory window. (We grew up in a boarding school environment)

I stole the shoes just to wear them and make a point to my school peers that I had some swag too. I lied to my family that

10

someone had been so kind as to give me the shoes. I searched for identity among peers and this made me want to please everyone so they would accept me. I never knew how to have a sensible debate or disagreement with anyone because I feared they would reject me and cast me out into the pit of ridicule and rejection. This made me a yes man. If you meet me today, I am not a yes man. I know who I am. I'm a child of God. I know what I believe, who I believe, what I stand for and what I do not stand for. I can have a meaningful argument, tell people off and carry myself with regal poise, so don't try me. Oh well, maybe some level of poise, hahaha, I'm a work in progress, okay! But I have been redeemed!

When I was younger, I easily started fights. I was so insecure, always wanted to prove something, but I was not a good fighter, so I always called on my big brother to show up and help, but many times he never did. I had to finish what I started; it wasn't good. I was too emotional, and I wasn't good at throwing punches, so I lost a lot of the fighting contests I initiated. I ended up with swollen lips, swollen eyes and shameful losses from fights I started. Looking back now, it was bad! Emotions may manipulate a situation for a minute, but they never win a fight or anything. If you picked on me today though, I might swing a few good punches and kicks and put up a really good argument while keeping my cool, so don't even start with me.....

The transforming power of Jesus Christ sets things right side up, turning weakness to strength and making wrong things right if we let Him. I have found that almost 100 percent of the things that stir up our emotions and trigger anger are not from outside of us. They are already inside of us. They are wounds inside that need to be healed and Jesus wants to heal our wounds, only if we let Him. Jesus wants to make us whole. I was wounded and carried my wounds around like there was a reward for them. This is how a victim mentality is built in us. The devil loves it that way because he can control us that way, but Jesus delivers us, gives us a reason not to carry our wounds around like trophies if we let Him. Jesus gives us His freedom. This is the freedom I have found in Him and continue to discover daily.

Apart from my mother making an effort to get us into good schools and make sure we had food to eat, plus being the tough disciplinarian, we did not have guidance on a lot of the issues in our lives. As I now say; We grew up by accident. I learned what sex was by accident and I started to explore it at a very young age even though I pretended not to know anything of it because I wanted to look like a really innocent kid, keeping up impressions.

Because I was embarrassed about my father, I never spoke of him at all in public. Every time someone said something about him or indicated I was his son, I felt small. I associated my dad with shame and embarrassment. If someone mistook me for a son of someone else I deemed more respectable, I took that as a compliment and quickly accepted it, hoping they wouldn't find out who I really was. Yes, I learned to keep up impressions early.

My high school years were chaotic. I was completely unstable; I was an average student too. My grades suffered due to my lack of identity. I was once last in a class of 40 students and I failed math at the senior 4 level high school national exam. To think that I'm a businessman today who works with numbers and makes a profit, it's ironic. Discovering who we really are directly affects our performance at everything else in life. I hungered for identity and wanted to be accepted and fit in so bad that it did not matter what I did, as long as the crew I wanted to fit in with did it. We sneaked out of school to smoke and drink, two things I was ashamed of my dad for doing and yet here I was repeating what I was ashamed of. Hypocrite, right! I must tell you, cigarette smoking hurt my chest and I wondered why anybody did it. But I still did it to fit in. A lack of identity can hurt your chest man.

Sneaking out of boarding school got me in trouble many times with the school administration and I had to report to the Headmaster's office. My friends knew how to lie their way out of trouble, but I spoke the truth, thinking it would earn me a way of escape from punishment. It never worked. It was my word against the majority. I got expelled from high school twice for being down with the clique and down on luck. Not a good look on a poor kid whose poor mother was trying her best with limited resources to help. I didn't see it that way then. I see it now. Because we were poor, my mother made chapatis (like tortillas only taste so much better). She baked cakes for sale to generate income for groceries. I was my mother's chief of sales from age 9.

Being the youngest in my family, I ended up doing all the house jobs my bigger siblings did not want to do. When I introduce myself to people these days as the youngest in my family, they say, "Oh, you were the baby, the spoiled one of the family." I say right back to them, I was the donkey of the family, so don't give me that baby stuff unless you want to fight, haha.

I was an average student, not because I was stupid, but because I was not very motivated. My hunger for identity far surpassed by my desire for good grades. By some miracle, I passed my national exams at all levels with distinctions in history, but failed math. In my last year of high school, I was a little more focused on good grades. I buried the issues inside and pretended they did not exist. I was involved in music, dance and drama in my last two years of high school and this made me a popular kid in a school of 3,000 plus students. The popularity gave me a sense of importance and value I had never experienced before.

Joyce Meyer once said, *"Your talent can take you where your character may not be able to sustain you."*

Well, she was right, as you will see in my story in the continuing chapters.

You cannot derive identity from your talent or from fans. True identity comes from inside you or you are just an empty shell thriving on outside energy, like one on drugs or alcohol. When the fans go and the drugs and alcohol cease their effect, you are back with your real self that you do not really like. Even with the popularity at school, I longed for something real. I felt a deep emotional void inside of me that I did not know how to fill. The high school fame was not filling it, the pretty girlfriend was not filling it, and she was very pretty too, I must tell you.

Deep inside, I was still this embarrassed and ashamed kid under the cover of talent and I did not fully know why or how to deal with it, but I wanted to deal with it.

They say fake it till you make it! Well, that doesn't work when you have deep emotional issues and wounds. You cannot fake healing and deliverance. You need an encounter with the life-giving energy of the Holy Spirit through Jesus Christ. Every person Jesus ever healed had to know they needed to be healed, believe they could be healed and believe Jesus could do it for them. That's why Jesus said to them, *"Your faith has healed you." (Mark 5:34)*

I believe the greatest healing miracle is not physical, but emotional. A redeemed, saved, sanctified, straightened out, transformed heart is life's greatest miracle.

After I completed high school in 1998, I felt a deep prophetic conviction in my heart that my life was about to change in a way I had never experienced before. I even spoke of it with a cousin as we discussed our New Year resolutions. A few months later, I gave my heart to Jesus and so the big astronomical shift of my life begun. This had been the deep conviction in my heart the whole time. God was drawing me to Himself. I must tell you, we grew up religious. My mother was a devout Catholic. Growing up, she made us go to church or else there would be no food. We had to go! After the new year celebrations in 1999, I moved to Kampala, Uganda's capital looking for opportunities which is what many young people in Uganda do. I met up with a cousin, Amos, who I had not seen for many years. He invited me to the church he

15

was going to for a service, and when I went, I instantly fell in love with the church because of the music.

Up to this point in my life, I did not know that church would be like that; Vibrant, lively with excellent singing. It felt unreal. I thought they were lip-syncing on stage. You see, my music background in high school was a lip-syncing star.

We imitated 3T's, New Edition, Boyz II Men, All 4 One etc. I was pretty sure they were lip-syncing too at the church. But, I noticed there was a full band on stage too and thought they couldn't all be pretending to do this. The drummer can't be pretending? That keyboard player cannot be pretending to play for sure. I was won over and thought to myself, I want to do this too. I kept coming back to the church that was Kampala Pentecostal Church then, now called Watoto Church. I resisted the call to salvation every time a challenge was made at the end of the service because I thought to myself, I cannot put my hand up with all these people looking, declaring I'm a sinner. I grew up going to church. I have not killed anyone, I'm not that bad or so I thought.

Religion tends to weigh the gravity of sin according to levels, but sin has no weighing scale. He who breaks one, breaks all. I was a broken, wounded sinner and I needed a healer, but my religious pride was standing in the way. I did not look at it that way then, but I do now. Religion can blind you and keep you in self-justification for things Jesus wants to set you free from.

For the person who keeps all of the laws except one is as guilty as a person who has broken all of God's laws.

(James 2:10)

I gave my heart to Jesus on Easter Sunday, April 4th, 1999. As always, I came to church that morning expectant. A convicting message on the death and resurrection of Christ was presented with humor and piercing truth. For the first time in my life, I did not care what anyone thought of me. For the first time in my life, I did not care who accepted me or if they thought I was a sinner, in which case they were right. I did not care. I was not here to keep up impressions anymore. I was going to accept Jesus. An alter call was made at the end of the service and I swiftly swung to my feet and walked to the front and, in tears, begun what has been the most important and meaningful relationship decision I ever made and anyone could ever make for themselves. I was born again. I had received a second chance at life. I would now start to learn to live my life in consultation with the author of life.

Very truly, I tell you, whoever hears my word and believes him who sent me has eternal life and will not be judged but has crossed over from death to life.

(John 5:24)

When I told my mother about my decision to give my heart to Jesus, she quickly rebuked me. She said I had made a big mistake. You see, my mother knew how unstable I was growing up. She thought in her mind this was another one of my impulsive and erratic decisions. She gave me five years to backslide. My sister argued that I was walking in rebellion to my parents, having made this decision and followed my own way away from the traditional Catholic way we were raised. You see, we might have grown up going to church, but we never lived as the church should. I lived my life any way I wanted and justified myself for attending church on Sunday. I climbed over roofs of buildings to break into disco halls for free. I got involved in fornication, masturbation, self-gratification, stealing, cheating and lying, but went to church on Sunday and felt justified.

I lived to please the flesh, as the Bible says. Something was missing and I knew it, and I wanted a quick fix without much as of a mess, cost or embarrassment to me. Don't we all want a quick, cost-free, problem-free fix in life? The truth is, transformation is messy! You are going to read about my transformation journey in the pages of this book.

My sister quoted scriptures at me on obeying and disobeying your parents and the consequences thereof to try and guilt me into backsliding. But I knew who I had believed and could not be persuaded otherwise. You see, on the day I gave my heart to Jesus, I had for the first time in my life felt a love I had never experienced before. A high and holy God who wanted a relationship with me, and with no strings attached. I had never experienced that before. This is the identity I had been searching for my whole life and did not know it. Up to this point, I had lived working hard to earn approval, but I did not need to earn this one. I had responded to unconditional love. Knowing this, I respectfully gave my mother five years to come to the same experience and fast forward five years later, God was working in my life in ways my family could not believe.

By now, I had joined the Watoto Choir as a chaperone/singer and had just finished a tour across the United Kingdom and was now continuing the tour in the United States. I called my mother to chat and the first thing she said to me was, she had received Jesus as her Lord and savior. This was exactly five years from the time my mother gave me five years to backslide and I had given her five years to come to know Jesus personally. I must tell you, I was not counting. This just happened as it did. God planned it that way. I rejoiced and forgot everything else I had planned to talk about in the phone call. My sister also encountered Jesus personally and we have become business and ministry partners. She helps me run a safari business I started and the business supports the Church I planted in 2014. I will be telling you more about my business and church planting journey in the chapters of this book. My mother is in Heaven now, so is my dad. I will share more on my dad's salvation journey ahead too.

I knew I was called to full-time ministry right after I got saved and at the earliest, I started to volunteer with the children's church as a facilitator. This ministry path led me to join Watoto Children's choir. The choir has been guests to the Whitehouse under President Bush, and the National Prayer Breakfast in Washington DC. They have also been to Buckingham Palace, parliament houses of nations among many important venues and churches around the globe. This was the beginning of my international adventures with Jesus. I served with the choir start of 2003 to December 2009.

My time with the choir took me to five continents of the world, sharing the story of hope in Jesus Christ and raising awareness and support for Uganda and Africa's orphans. The once air-conditioned clothes guy, who could not even make a trip to the airport, was now traveling in air-conditioned airplanes, living in air-conditioned houses, globetrotting. Not a big deal for some born in affluence, but this was a big deal for me and still is. We should never get so used to God's goodness that we take Him for granted. I am not there yet, but I am daily learning to live with gratitude even with the frustrations and delays and trials that accompany my life of faith. I can't believe I'm even saying that because I have much to be grateful to God for.

I have come to the conclusion looking at my own life, that no matter what happens, God is good and He has good plans and makes all things work together for our good if we love Him. Where you are born, what family you are born in is not a disadvantage to God. In fact, it is an opportunity for God to reveal His glory. Our lives are like the man born blind that Jesus healed;

> Now, as Jesus was passing by, He saw a man blind from birth, and His disciples asked Him, "Rabbi, who sinned, this man or his parents, that he was born blind?" Jesus answered, "Neither this man nor his parents sinned, but this happened so that the works of God would be displayed in him.
>
> **(John 9:1-3)**

We were born where we were, as we were, so that the glory of God would be revealed in us and through our lives. No matter the seeming limitations, the failures and challenges we encounter in this life, God's love is constant, and He makes all things work out for His glory if we trust Him in faith. God is not waiting for you to give your heart to Jesus and change so He can love you. God decided to love us way before we ever knew of Him or thought of Him. God loves all 7 billion plus humans on planet earth, but it is those who respond to and open up to His love that experience His unconditional, unfailing, astronomical love. It is God's love and kindness that draws us to Jesus. God accepts us as we are, but He will never leave us as we are. God's love is liberating, transforming, healing, delivering, freeing and all the beautiful things genuine, unconditional love is.

As I continue telling my story, I would like to give you reading this an opportunity to start the most wonderful life-changing relationship; A relationship with Christ Jesus, if you have not started one yet. Please pray this prayer;

> *Lord Jesus, I am a sinner. I have failed You. I have failed myself and failed Heaven. I have lived for myself and not for Your glory. Forgive me of my sin, come into my heart, be my Lord and my Savior. Help me to live for You from this day onwards. I receive You now with a thankful heart. In Your most beautiful name, Amen!*

> *If you declare with your mouth, 'Jesus is Lord,' and believe in your heart that God raised Him from the dead, you will be saved.*

> **(Romans 10:9)**

Friends, this is how I started my journey with the Creator of the universe. This is how I made the best decision of my life ever. If you have prayed this prayer and mean it, I would like to hear from you. Please send me an email using the address I will indicate at the end of the book. Also, I encourage you to find an all of the Bible-believing, life-giving, God-fearing, Christ-centered church near you and join the largest family on planet earth. Start learning, get involved in serving in any capacity so you can grow and discover your purpose on earth for the Kingdom.

Chapter 1

The Calling

M any people often wonder about their calling in life. I cannot tell you what your calling is, but I can share my own experience and hopefully, you can get some insight for your own journey. A calling is not a career. It is much deeper and greater than the advancement of self. God calls people in different ways. Everyone's calling is cut to the continuity of the gifts God has placed within them. There is no one-size-fits-all. Each one is called according to his or her ability. According to what God already placed inside of you to be and to do in this world. You cannot copy your purpose. It is given to you and discovered by you as you follow God in faith.

> *To one, he gave five bags of gold, to another two bags, and to another one bag, each according to his ability. Then he went on his journey.*

> **(Matthew 25:15)**

The overarching factor in discovering your calling is a desire and hunger for the things of God. If you are hungry for the things of God, you will discover your calling because it flows out of the intimacy of the relationship you cultivate with God. You must avail yourself to serve in any capacity in ministry if you are looking to discover your calling. Your calling is not a position to fill, but a unique role to play in God's giant story for mankind. No one else can be who God wants you to be. In fact, no one can teach you what your true calling is. A leader can guide you, but it is revealed and unveiled from within as you trust and follow God in obedience and faith. If you do not discover your calling and live it out, there will always be a gap in your place in history. God is counting on you and I to discover our calling. You say what? God is counting on me? Yes, He is. God is counting on you to seek Him with all your heart so you can discover all the things He has in store for you to be and to do. Your calling will not be handed to you. It is discovered, so you must start somewhere and seek to live for God faithfully. Not perfectly, but faithfully. Being faithful is being your best for God at all times. It is having an excellent spirit and doing everything with excellence, to the best of your ability.

> *Then you will call on me and come and pray to me, and I will listen to you. You will seek me and find me when you seek me with all your heart.*

> **(Jeremiah 29:12-13)**

When I felt a calling to full-time ministry, I knew I had to start somewhere, so I found a need at Children's church for a facilitator and that's where it all started for me. You are not going to hear a voice from Heaven giving you a specific role like, "Hey Pumba, you are called to be an usher or preacher." Like I once heard Robert Barriger say in a sermon at a Hillsong Conference, *"You don't have to copy someone. Just find an itch and scratch it."*

Start with what's available to do that needs to be done and what you do will become definitive as you go.

We all know Saul, the guy who became Paul as the guy who persecuted the church, whose life was turned around and who became a pillar in the early church. Well, Paul's role in the church became defined as he went. It was not defined the day he encountered Jesus. Paul, on the road to Damascus, encountered the living Christ and was blinded by a bright light. The Lord Jesus asked him why he was persecuting Him. Paul seemed to already know who the real LORD was because he responded with who are you, LORD? When Christ appears to you, there will be no mistaking who He is. Christ, in that moment, called Paul to serve Him.

> *Meanwhile, Saul was still breathing out murderous threats against the Lord's disciples. He went to the high priest and asked him for letters to the synagogues in Damascus, so that if he found any there who belonged to the Way, whether men or women, he might take them as prisoners to Jerusalem. As he neared Damascus on his journey, suddenly, a light from heaven flashed around him. He fell to the ground and heard a voice say to him, "Saul, Saul, why do you persecute me?" "Who are you, Lord?" Saul asked. "I am Jesus, whom you are*

persecuting," he replied. "Now get up and go into the city, and you will be told what you must do."

(Acts 9:1-6)

There were no specifics to Paul, like you will be an Apostle, planting churches, healing people, preaching the gospel. Paul had been called. The rest was up to Paul to discover and he had to go at it with all his heart, to be bold and courageous to get that done. You need to be courageous if you are going to discover your purpose. If you feel like you have done a lot of bad things and do not qualify to be serving in ministry, well, look at brother Paul, look at me, look at us! I was not very confident when I started to get involved in ministry. In fact, when I was introduced to the person who was going to be my immediate supervisor in children's church ministry, I trembled inside with the unhealthy, insecure fear of unworthiness. It was bad. You must be willing to take risks even when you are afraid or feel unqualified. Get involved even when fear says you are not worthy to serve. Jesus qualifies the worst of us. You ought to get out of familiar environments that have kept you living for yourself and risk ridicule taking steps of faith if you are going to walk in God's purpose for you. You must say yes to God and keep saying yes, even when things get tough, when you feel inadequate and when things start to not make sense as you go.

But the Lord said to Ananias, 'Go! This man is my chosen instrument to proclaim my name to the Gentiles and their kings and to the people of Israel.

I will show him how much he must suffer for my name.'

(Acts 9:15-16)

Show him what? How much he must suffer for me! Wait a minute, Lord! I thought you called Paul to be an Apostle, to preach the gospel, wasn't that his calling? Yes, plus suffering. Many people miss their calling because they are looking for convenience and comfort. In order to fulfill your calling in the Kingdom, you must be willing to give up a lot of your own preferences and comforts and make the sometimes inconvenient things of God a priority. There is nothing convenient about serving Heaven's purposes on earth. In the same breathe, there is nothing more fulfilling than finding and serving your God-given purpose. Fulfillment is found in the middle of the discomfort and inconvenience of doing God's will for you.

> *Whoever does not take up their cross and follow me is not worthy of me. Whoever finds their life will lose it, and whoever loses their life for my sake will find it.*

(Matthew 10:38-39)

Right place!

My ministry adventures started with volunteering in Children's church as a facilitator and evolved from joining the world-renowned Watoto Choir to becoming a worship leader and pastor/church planter today. Everything has unfolded organically. Start somewhere and stay faithfully planted. God will lead you.

The call to join the choir came when I was already involved in active ministry in children's church, so I was known as an active, faithful individual in ministry already. I was in the right place at the right time, doing the right thing for the transition to happen in the progression of my ministry journey. You must be willing to start somewhere, anywhere and despise not any role if you are going to walk in your calling. I am a church planter today, but I started as a children's church volunteer and stayed where God asked me to stay until He moved me. God will only guide you if you get moving. You could never navigate a car that is in neutral could you? Waiting for the ideal moment and not committing to anything because you are waiting for that moment has hindered many people from walking in God's purpose for them. There will never be an ideal moment. Start now; commit now.

The good thing about God is, He is patient. When you are ready to start, however long you have procrastinated, He will work with you and guide you and show you the way. It is never too late to start pursuing your calling, no matter how old you are and how much you have delayed starting. It's never too late to start somewhere and let God lead you. Making yourself available to serve in any capacity is always the right place with God. Besides, God can fast forward our process no matter what level we start at depending on our level of commitment to Him.

'Who dares despise the day of small things?"

(Zechariah 4:10)

Risking it all!

Pursuing your calling is going to require a considerable level of risk on your part. My journey started with the desire and availability to do what was required and available to do. It evolved into taking risks in pursuit of my calling away from the predictable. What you are doing in ministry today will eventually become predictable and God will ask you to move on, or He will make it uncomfortable for you to stay in it so that you can move forward to the unpredictable place that requires faith.

We walk by faith and not by sight.

(2 Corinthians 5:7)

When I got offered the opportunity to join the Watoto Choir, I was just about to receive my first salary in a new job I had been at hardly a month. The opportunity I was being offered with the choir was as a volunteer and there was no guarantee that I would keep the role. It was made clear to me from the onset that this was going to be on a trial basis to see if my personality and my work ethic fit with the rest of the team. Plus, there was no pay, just a small monthly allowance eight times less than my first salary. I had to decide whether to stay in a new, somewhat secure and predictable job with reasonable pay or take the new ministry opportunity with a considerable pay cut coupled with the uncertainty of not being sure I would make the team.

Any one of us would want to ask God to confirm if this was indeed what they were meant to do. I mean, if you are coming from a poor background, have struggled financially all your life and finally have some semblance of financial security, you do not want to throw that away easy, do you? I cannot tell you how to know what decision to make when you encounter such a scenario. What I can tell you is, your priorities will determine your decisions. Fulfilling my purpose in God was and is much more appealing than financial security. As I mentioned earlier, when I gave my heart to Jesus, I knew right away that I was called to full-time ministry. When God is leading you, there will often be a prompting in your spirit, a sense of excitement and deep inner peace mixed with a sense of fear. In my experience, I have found that the things of God often present themselves with a sense of excitement about the possibilities and fear because of the uncertainties. You are excited about the possibilities, but you are not sure how it will all pan out, so you fear. When you give yourself to it fully without holding back, in the excitement, the fear and all, you are on track to discovering God's purpose. Jentezen Franklin, one of my favorite preachers, once said, *"Faith is spelled R.I.S.K."*

The disciples risked everything to follow Jesus. Their very livelihood was on the line. The calling of God will always present itself to you when you have options. God and laziness do not go together, because lazy folks have nothing to give. All the disciples gave up something they were doing to follow Jesus. God wants to know if He is a priority to you and if the things of the Kingdom are worth taking a risk on for you. That is why God will sometimes be silent when you have to make a decision to serve Him. It is because He wants it to be your decision, one you voluntarily and willingly took on, forsaking all other paths because you love Jesus and consider Heaven's purpose for you more important than anything else. Pursuing your calling is somewhat similar to marriage; Forsaking all others, you choose the one path. No wonder the church of Christ is called the bride of Christ.

Risking everything for the sake of the Kingdom does not mean everything will automatically fall in line and flow smoothly because you sincerely chose to pursue the calling of God on your life. There will always be a degree of uncertainty and fear going with the risks you take. This is what will always bring us to a place of surrender, depending on God and not leaning on our own understanding. There is a Kingdom reward that comes only with risking everything for the sake of the Kingdom. Christ's disciples experienced their own fears after they left everything to follow Him.

> *Then Peter spoke up, "We have left everything to follow you!" "Truly I tell you," Jesus replied, "no one who has left home or brothers or sisters or mother or father or children or fields for me and the gospel will fail to receive a hundred times as much in this present age: homes, brothers, sisters, mothers, children and fields–along with persecutions–and in the age to come eternal life.*

> **(Mark 10:28-30)**

What started as a risk, a trial period for me, turned into seven years of traveling the world, sharing the message of hope, raising awareness and support for Uganda's AIDS orphans, in an experience that turned my life around. I served as a caregiver to the kids, as a singer, a sound guy, set up and tear down crew and then as team leader/pastor for my last two years. The organization has thus far rescued over 5,000 children, some of them former child soldiers in northern Uganda.

Towards the end of the seven years, God said to me, you have been on this mountain long enough; time to move on. What was I going to fall back on? Nothing? Just to start from scratch again, to take another risk in continuous pursuit of my calling. Bishop T. D Jakes calls it starting from one again on another level. You can be a big ten on a lower level or you can start again and continue to 11 on another level but which will feel like a completely fresh start.

I know someone is still asking, 'How did you really know it was time to move on?" God said it! God speaks to me in promptings, in dreams. He interferes with our thoughts by dropping in a word that leads us to seek out more information.

In my case, while I was considering leaving my seven-year world travel ministry opportunity, I called a friend of mine and the first thing he said without me sharing a word about my intentions was, "It's time for you to move on and do other things." He kept on talking about what I could possibly do and went on and on and on, trying to convince me before I stopped him and said I had already made the decision to move on. God was leading me to. Confirmation! God will confirm His intentions for you with other people, but it will always be up to you to take the risk. So if you are not sure, God will confirm His intentions through someone else.

So I resigned from my job, the best opportunity I had ever had in my life to that point. My non-believing brothers said I was a fool to quit that kind of opportunity, but I thought to myself, God gave me this opportunity, He can take it back, He will always have another one for me. When God asks you to move on, don't insist on staying, you will miss out on what He has prepared ahead and you will be occupying someone else's place while yours is vacant up ahead.

Ministry in disguise

When I quit my job, I had little to fall back on. I had spent most of my savings building a house for my parents, so this was a step of faith. I took what I had left in the bank and paid up rent for my apartment for six months in advance. I figured if I went hungry, at least I would have a roof over my head for six months.

I registered a company - Border-Less Travel, which focused on hosting tourists to East Africa. I said to God in that time, 'Father, I thought I was called to full-time ministry? This is not ministry!" God said to me, "It is. You will discover it later. Just keep going, son."

The first four months figuring things out after leaving my good job was a struggle. And just when I was about to register my first clients, my website got switched off because I could not pay to renew the hosting. It wasn't much, but I couldn't afford it. I thought that was the last straw in all my struggles, but a few days later, I received a phone call from an anonymous number and someone speaking in a European accent. They asked to speak to Peter and I said, "speaking." They then went on to remind me my website was not working and my emails were bouncing back. I thought to make up a story to explain why, but then I decided I'll be honest. The things of God do not require tricks to work. I said to the guy, my website hosting expired. That's why it is not working and that's why emails are bouncing back. The same company hosts my emails too. I thought he was going to hang up on me and say, shady dealer! But he went on to ask if I had an alternative email address. I gave him my Gmail address, thinking no way in the world he was going to write me or book a trip with me considering the shady-looking circumstances. To my surprise, he wrote me an email saying he still wanted to book the trip. I still did not believe him, so I jokingly asked him to make a deposit if he really wanted to book the trip. He asked how he would make the deposit, I said through a bank transfer. He asked for the bank details, which I sent to him, but I was still not sure he was for real. I found out three days later he was for real because he had transferred several thousand dollars into my business account. I knew this was an act of God. Website down, emails down, who books their long-awaited, once in a lifetime three-week holiday trip with a company like that? God does!

Nobody books a trip to a country they have never been to with a company whose emails are not working and whose website has been switched off. This was a miracle! They came a month later. I took them on their 21 days safari, which they enjoyed thoroughly. This is when it dawned on me that I was doing involuntary worship. I was taking people to wow at God's creation. They praise Him by marveling at His creation and them without knowing it. This too was ministry!

By the word of the Lord, the heavens were made, their starry host by the breath of his mouth. He gathers the waters of the sea into jars; he puts the deep into storehouses. Let all the earth fear the Lord; let all the people of the world revere him. For he spoke, and it came to be; he commanded, and it stood firm.

(Psalms 33:6-9)

My business started to attract more customers based on the good recommendation of the first ones. I offered the best service possible, going above and beyond what my clients expected.

Just because God has given you an opportunity doesn't mean favor will fix everything. You have to do your part like Joshua. Be diligent, be strategic, be friendly and hospitable, create good impressions then leave it all in God's hands. You have to work your calling because God will not work it for you. Whatever God leads you to do; A job, a business, it is stewardship. He is expecting nothing but your best effort. Our effort may not be perfect, but it has to be the best we can put in. It's all God accepts and rewards.

Whatever you do, work at it with all your heart, as working for the Lord, not for human masters, since you know that you will receive an inheritance from the Lord as a reward. It is the Lord Christ you are serving.

(Colossians 3:23-24)

Planting a church

After three years in the safari business, I felt God tagging at my heart to focus on planting a church back in my hometown in Eastern Uganda - Mbale, a city I have since dubbed "the most happening town." It's a little city with a population of about 140,000 people and it is the place I was born. I dream of the day that 40% of the population of this city will be members of our church. The calling to focus on planting a church came at a time of mourning. My mother had just had a stroke, and my dad had just passed away. This all happened within a space of two weeks. Now I told you before that I grew up embarrassed about my earthly father and wished I was an orphan. Well, when he died, I did not feel the same way, God had redeemed our relationship and I will share more about the beautiful healing story of redemption between my dad and myself in the next chapter, so don't touch that dial, lol!

God said to me at that time of mourning, "When are you going to start?" I said, "Start what?" He said the church. You see, in 2007, whilst participating in one of Hillsong Church conferences in Sydney, Australia, I was so amazed at the size of the gathering of thousands of Christians under one roof singing praises to our God. I thought to myself, I will one day go back to my home town and plant a church and maybe God can do something really big with it because God is no respecter of persons. Fast forward to six years later and God was asking.

When are you going to start the church? This was a six-year conversation. God was responding to my thoughts from 2007. Sometimes we miss God's answers because we are in a hurry while God is about a process. I said to God, "Can't you see we are mourning? These are sad times, Sir!" But God insisted, when are you going to start? So I said to God, I thought you would give me a date to start.

Besides, we are still mourning. God then said to me, "You are not going to have this life for long. You, too, will die one day. The question is, while you still have this life, what are you going to do with it? Life is short, son, so get over your mourning and get planning for the church." Sounds crass, doesn't it? Kind of like, *"Let the dead bury their own dead." (Luke 9:60)* or *"The poor you will always have with you." (Matthew 26:11) or "You do not take the children's bread and toss it to dogs." (Matthew 15:26)*

But still, I asked God, when do we start? I got no response. That's when I decided I was going to set a date and start a church. God is short on details. He is not going to tell you everything you want to hear about what He is calling you to do. After all, we walk by faith and not by sight. Plus, He wants you to own what He calls you to do. So I set a date; January 26th, 2014, we would start Musaale Church. Musaale means friend. Jesus is a friend of sinners.

When I set out to plant the church, I needed resources. I needed funds to make this happen. I did not have to look too far. I had all the money I needed to launch the church and to keep it going because God had blessed my business. I became like Paul; My safari company was my tent-making business to support my Kingdom ventures. Earlier I mentioned that I asked God why I was leaving full-time ministry, and He said to me that my business was my ministry. Well, my business certainly helped us get the church planted and going. The church has now grown to two campuses. The second one is in Soroti, a town 60 miles north of Mbale.

When I went back to my hometown to start the church, at first, I thought to myself, "God, why do we need another church? There are a lot of churches here already." I have since learned that when God calls you to plant a church, He is asking you to plant an expression of His heart and your relationship with Him to the people who will come. Not a place that follows programs, but a place where Heaven collides with earth. If the church was a social club, then there are already too many.

A visit from Heaven

One day after I set the date for the launching of Musaale church, I was fasting on a Friday and also had an appointment to visit my pastor at Watoto Church to share with him about my intentions to plant a church in my hometown. After I shared my heart and intentions, he blessed me and wished me the best. That night while asleep, I had a dream that was more like a vision. In it I saw a rainbow and as I looked around, rainbows kept appearing, I counted them and there were seven rainbows in total. While I was still marveling at the rainbows, I looked up and the heavens were lit up with stars.

It was clear as day on the ground where I stood, but the skies were dark as night covered in the shining of the stars. I saw a shooting star and what appeared like a human shadow descend out of it. Before I knew it, I was carried away in what was an out-of-body experience and taken flying. We sat on what was like a mound. I could see the hands of the one holding me in his lap, but could not see his face. I was sitting in his lap like children sit in their father's lap.

I still cannot describe what his hands looked like, but the form was like our human form. It's just that his body was made of something totally different. It glittered like diamonds and sort of looked like Lapis Lazuli, for lack of a better description. I asked him who held me in his laps, who he was and where he came from. He said to me in the cleanest English accent I have ever heard, "I come from where eagles fly. I have been sent by Jesus." After our conversion, I was back in my bed and that is when I woke up with a fire burning inside of me. Heaven had just visited me and filled me with fire. I still get the same fire burning inside me when I talk about the experience. In fact, I'm feeling the fire right now. It has never stopped burning within me. I knew that day that Jesus was confirming my calling to go and plant the church. John the Baptist said there comes one after me who will baptize you with fire, well I had been baptized with fire. Jesus said to His disciples;

> *But you will receive power when the Holy Spirit comes on you; and you will be my witnesses in*
>
> *Jerusalem, and in all Judea and Samaria, and to the ends of the earth."*

(Acts 1:8)

Before we embark on a mission for the Kingdom, it is important that we are set on fire by the Holy Spirit. The fire will sustain you and be a reassuring and empowering presence in you when you face discouragement on the mission.

I wish I could say that all my fears and insecurities and doubts and weaknesses faded at that moment when I was set on fire, but no, I was still struggling with fears, doubts and insecurities. But that presence is always burning inside me, reminding me who I am and that my mission on earth is important. It represents Heaven in me. The presence of God in our lives does not remove human weakness. It becomes our power to prevail in spite of weakness. I believe the fire is what it means to have the tangible presence of Heaven living inside of us on earth. It is what causes us to touch others with the same fire that has touched us and lives in us. The same power that raised Christ from the dead lives in us.

When we launched Musaale church, I was excited and scared. Part of me thought we were bringing a new church culture. God had asked me to plant this church, so people will come flocking in to experience the life we were bringing, God will send them surely or He wouldn't ask me to plant the church. They will come in droves, I thought. That wasn't the case at all. I discovered people were not as enthusiastic as I was about the new church plant. If anything, they were suspicious of my dream! The first service had 26 people in attendance and most of them were my relatives. The next Sunday, 7 people, and on and on, we had 5, 8, 7, 10 in attendance. It was discouraging until God said to me one day; Who are you doing this for? People or me? I'm always in the service, sing to me son, celebrate my presence, I AM always with you. This changed my whole perspective on what I was doing and what planting a church meant. God does not just call us to ministry. He calls us to Himself. When I ceased to care too much about people coming, God started sending them. People started to come in and gave their hearts to Jesus, plus they committed to being part of the house. Some recommitted their lives. Others God sent to be part of the ministry.

18 months after we planted Musaale church in the most happening place, God said to plant a second campus in Soroti. I said we are not ready, God! We need time to build some sort of capacity here. As it is, we are still growing a team here. God said, you are ready, son, so get going. God does not call you according to what you know or see, but according to what He knows and sees, and He's got a much better view of things than we do. I kept going back and forth with God. We are not ready. You are ready! Until one day, as I got up from bed, I heard a voice directing me to someone in the town where God said to plant the church. The voice said, "You have Mike!" God will never give you what you can handle. He gives you what you can trust Him to handle for you, with you, through you.

I said to God, I do not know Mike. There was silence. I later figured out who Mike was, a guy I had worked with at Watoto, who had relocated to Soroti, his hometown at the call of God. When I went to meet Mike, he was looking for a life-giving church, plus he had a team of people with him ready to get involved in a life-giving church. Long story short, at the instruction of God, we started a second campus in Soroti with a ready team. Both campuses have about 350 adults and children combined. One day we will have tens of thousands coming, but my focus has never been numbers. It always has and will always be character. Organic growth where people get to experience and witness what the character of Christ looks like to the point they want that for themselves. That's what the church is all about. We are called to make disciples, not churchgoers. Jesus is attractive and when He is represented well, many want to be like Him.

> Then Jesus came to them and said, "All authority in heaven and on earth has been given to me. Therefore go and make disciples of all nations, baptizing them in the name of the Father and of the Son and of the Holy Spirit, and teaching them to obey everything I have commanded you. And surely I am with you always, to the very end of the age."

> **(Matthew 28:18-20)**

The church was never about numbers alone. It was and will always be about disciples in large numbers. People who have laid down their lives for the sake of the Kingdom. As I write the pages of this book, I'm in the United States continuing my mission with God exploring planting a life-giving church in this part of the world. I have been to many parts of the world, five continents in all and traveled to 44 states across America + two I just went through on a train recently. I always felt a calling to be involved in the church in America in some way from the first time I came out on tour with the Watoto choir.

In 2019, God kept tagging at my heart to delegate my pastoral responsibilities, to sit back and see the progress of my leaders. At first, I thought, why? But God insisted on the challenge. I needed to step aside and see if things wouldn't happen without me. I am a very hands-on person, so it takes a bit of convincing to get me to do nothing, but I did. I started showing up to attend church, give some advice and started to enjoy it too. I knew God was working in the house and could use anyone who has a heart for Him to steward what He started.

At the end of 2019, God said to me, get up and go to the United States and let's explore the next chapter. It's easy to walk by faith when going to the next town. But walking by faith to a whole other country thousands of miles away, that's a whole other thing. I was like Gideon, wanting to make sure God was leading me. I said to put out a fleece overnight, but God said, stop it, son! That was for Gideon. Now get going. 2019 was a hard year for my business, so I was not sure how I was going to afford to make the trip. We had a booking just in time and made enough profit to buy me a ticket and a little extra.

I booked a ticket to Los Angeles and did not make any arrangements with anyone. I figured if God has sent me, He will have someone waiting with my name at the arrivals, even an Angel. Well, there was no one. I quickly figured I needed to do something or I would sleep in the airport seats. I found a place for the night, then the next day a place in Norwalk, California to stay for a while with people I had met only once whose daughter is a member of my church in Uganda. I spent most of 2020 in central Florida, exploring to plant a life-giving church. I wish the things of God were straightforward, from A to B, but they are not. I'm in the state of Maryland as I write this continuing on my journey with the Holy Spirit.

Trusting God by faith and following His lead, never have I gone hungry or lacked a place to rest my head. God has provided through complete strangers. It is easy to think that the people you already know will be the first to support your mission, but the people who know you may not even believe your mission. When God calls us to walk by faith, He will confirm our calling by providing for us through anyone, complete strangers, kind of like God used Ravens to feed Elijah. I'm still exploring, waiting on God for what He has for me to do in this nation even as I connect with people, pray with and for people, lead in Bible studies and share wherever I am invited to speak. I know I'm right where I need to be for such a time as this. I look forward to what God and I will do as I invest my little 5 cents worth towards the church in the United States of America. I look forward to spending my years between Uganda and the United States, plus wherever else God will call me.

"God will never give you what you can handle. He gives you what you can trust Him to handle in you, with you, through you."

Chapter 2

Redemption

For God so loved the world that he gave his one and only Son, that whoever believes in him shall not perish but have eternal life. For God did not send his Son into the world to condemn the world, but to save the world through him.

(John 3:16-17)

I know you may have heard this scripture a zillion times and could even say it in your sleep. You may also be one of those who haven't heard of it. I want to share with you how God made this verse portion of the Bible come alive for me. You see, it is one thing to quote scripture and a whole other thing for scripture to come alive in you and for you in a truly applicable and life-changing fashion. The Bible is the only book that reads us while we read it.

When I gave my heart to Jesus, I knew I was called to full-time ministry. I thought it was my job to get other people saved. I later discovered that I was only partly right about this. We preach to people. We love them genuinely and sincerely. The Holy Spirit does the convicting and saving. We are but delivery boys and girls.

When I started to share with people about my faith in Jesus, about the unconditional love, I had experienced, and the fact that they could be saved too, some laughed at me, others mocked me. I had naively thought quoting scripture at people was supposed to slay them. I knew whom I had believed, what I felt inside and thought to myself, everyone needs to have this life-changing experience. I tried this on my alcoholic dad for a long time and at times, it looked like I was getting to him with my message, but it never worked. I couldn't save my dad. I was frustrated.

I shared earlier that my dad was an alcoholic and how that affected my siblings and me. One day, my dad got sick and I went over to his house to take him to the hospital. I did not preach to him. In fact, I had stopped preaching to him altogether. God had been teaching me about John 3:16 from His viewpoint. You see, I preached to my dad because I wanted him to stop drinking. I thought once he got saved, he would be fixed, shame and embarrassment would cease. I was trying to fix my dad. I preached to him because I wanted him to change so he would cease to be an embarrassment to me. This was all about what I wanted and not to share the love of God with and for him. We cannot use the Bible to fix people. We are called to love them, and God fixes them. God showed me that I was still carrying my childhood shame and embarrassment and anger towards my dad. These things were hindering the working of the Holy Spirit and undermining my ministry impact not just with my dad, but in other areas of ministry in my life.

That day in the hospital, I asked to talk to him. I needed to bring all the shame and embarrassment out to the light. I said to my dad; You know, growing up, we were embarrassed about you because of your drinking that caused many in the community to ridicule us, call us good for nothing, will never amount to much in life. I was ashamed of you and I wished I was an orphan. Can you forgive me for ever holding such thoughts towards you, because it doesn't matter what you did with your life, you were still my father and I had no right to think that way about you. He simply nodded in acknowledgment. He did not say a thing back to me. My dad was a man of few words.

When he left the hospital three days later, he said he was never going to drink again. "Why," his brothers asked? "Because it embarrassed my children," he said. True to his word, he experienced an overnight deliverance from alcohol. There was no rehab and no medicine for withdrawals. It was a miracle! Things even got better; My dad started reading the Bible for himself. By now, I knew my job was to love him because God so loved us. I knew I could not save my dad, but God could. I knew that my dad would not get saved just for my sake, but for his own sake and for the sake of the finished work of Christ.

One day when I went to visit him at his house, I did not preach a word, just went to visit and deliver a gift. He asked me to pray with him. I was surprised because he had never been interested, so I asked why. He said because he believed.

He had read his Bible and he believed. You see, I did not give him that Bible. But I had prayed that someone would, anyone. So I probed to see where he was. Do you believe what is written in the Bible? Believe God loves you and has good plans for you and wants you to spend eternity in Heaven with Him? He nodded yes. So on that day, I prayed with my dad, led him in the prayer of salvation and then begun the redemption of my relationship with my earthly father.

We can love people into the Kingdom or we can give them the condemning law seeking to correct them, but instead push them farther away from wanting anything to do with Jesus. We must be truthful and honest and present the gospel as is, but we must share the truth in love, with the other person's best interest at heart. This is why God sent Jesus. He had our best interest at heart.

My dad died four months later, and I was not happy. I said to God, why? We were just starting to have something wonderful. The earthly father I only ever dreamed of having was coming alive and now this? I wanted my dad alive. It dawned on me at that moment what redemption means. I had experienced it in my relationship with my earthly father. The man I grew up embarrassed and ashamed of most of my life started to call me to pray with me. He started to become my good friend. I started to be proud of him. Shame and embarrassment was being replaced with pride. I knew then firsthand that there is no such thing as beyond repair when it comes to God. He will repair even the worst of relationships and most hopeless of situations if we give Him a chance. The key thing is to give God a chance. Nothing is irredeemable with God.

Just when humanity was irredeemable, God sent Jesus to the cross because He so loved us. The gospel is best propagated effectively when we love people with God's kind of love, when we have their best interest at heart. You cannot use the gospel for your personal agenda. It has to be for Kingdom agenda.

> *Very rarely will anyone die for a righteous person, though for a good person someone might possibly dare to die. But God demonstrates his own love for us in this: While we were still sinners, Christ died for us.*
>
> **(Romans 5:7-8)**

My dad is in Heaven now with Jesus and I will see him one day. There's one of two places we end up after this life: Heaven or hell. The only way to Heaven is through receiving Jesus as your Lord and Savior. You can never be good enough to be admitted to Heaven. Only the name of Jesus can save you and bring you into the presence of Almighty God. It's never too late to receive Jesus too. Just say, Jesus, I need You, save me!

Wake up call!

> *But everything exposed by the light becomes visible—and everything that is illuminated becomes a light. This is why it is said: "Wake up, sleeper, rise from the dead, and Christ will shine on you." Be very careful, then, how you live—not as unwise but as wise, making the most of every opportunity, because*

the days are evil. Therefore do not be foolish, but understand what the Lord's will is.

(Ephesians 5:13-17)

I want to share with you another aspect of my redemption story. When God takes us on a journey of redemption, He leaves no stone unturned. God will go into the details of our lives if we let Him and He will set everything right side up. When I gave my heart to Jesus, I did not know just how much I needed to be saved, or how dysfunctional I was. Religion has a way of fooling us into embracing and justifying our dysfunction as our normal. The devil likes that because he can control us that way. When God takes us on a journey of light that reveals us to ourselves in comparison to Him, it awakens us to who we can be in Him. God never compares us to someone else. Some people feel comfortable in their dysfunction because they are better than someone else, but our standard is not another person. It is Jesus Christ. God reveals us in stages as we grow and as He slowly wins us to Himself. The Bible is called the living word because as you read it, it reads you. I mentioned in the introduction that I pretty much grew up by accident. When it came to things like sex, I figured that out by accident. I discovered sex through curiosity and engaged in the practice from a very young age. I still pretended to be an innocent kid who knew nothing of the sort. I could have fooled you.

I discovered masturbation in my early teenage years when I started to become insecure and fear girls because of some of the things I was discovering about my teenage self. I had a skin infection called ringworm which my dad had. I inherited that from him, but have since disinherited it. It made me feel very insecure about my physical appearance as a teenager, even later. One day I stumbled on a pornographic image in an internet cafe and was hooked. I continued to watch pornography and practice masturbation even after I gave my heart to Jesus until one day, God got my attention. He said to me if you continue with these things, there's very little I will be able to do with you. In fact, it all happened when I was given a ministry promotion that I lost, because God said NO! God said to me; We cannot do much together at a higher level in what you call ministry until you take ME seriously, son." You cannot live how you want, gratifying the flesh and still get to represent ME.

Losing the promotion was a wake-up call. I had worked so hard to earn it and thought I deserved it. You see, in a secular environment, I was certainly deserving of the promotion because I had earned it. But that is not how it works in the Kingdom. Working so hard doesn't count as much as living faithfully and obediently in God's eyes; he wants both. Working diligently and not allowing yourself to be mastered by selfish, self-gratifying desires. Serving faithfully in ministry without devotion to God in your secret life will not earn you any points with God. You might as well be part of a social club.

> Do not get drunk on wine, which leads to debauchery. Instead, be filled with the Spirit.

> **(Ephesians 5:18)**

Wine is used here as the reference, but you could be full of anything that stands in the way of God. It could be food, sexual sin, alcohol, drugs, a job, anger, someone you are obsessed with etc. This scripture calls us to derive our sense of satisfaction and contentment in and from God and nothing else. To be satisfied with spiritual food! Jesus said He is the bread of life. When we take Holy Communion, it is a physical dramatization of what should be a spiritual reality in our lives. We are daily being filled with the life-giving, redeeming power and presence of Jesus.

When God started to awaken me to my reality, a bright light had just been switched on in my life and I realized at that moment that I had settled for a very shallow experience with God. In fact, I was in charge and He wasn't, even though I claimed He was in charge. I was what they call a carnal Christian, consumed by the lust of the flesh. My bell had been rung. The light had been turned on. It wasn't going to be business as usual unless I continued in my ways.

After the lost ministry promotion, I started to invest in my relationship with God and make Him a priority. The experience was humiliating and sobering. For the first time up to this point, I realized my spiritual apathy. I wept over my spiritual condition, I repented and made some resolutions; That I would invest in my relationship with Jesus first and foremost. Regular church attendance, even regular prayer and fellowship meetings were not going to cut it. If this was going to happen, I needed to give my whole life as a living sacrifice. I often tell people in my church that it is not enough to come to church on Sunday. You have to invest yourself in pursuing God on your own. You have to own your spiritual journey and growth or you will course on neutral and that's dangerous and ineffective. I say that because I learned it from personal experience. Attending church programs and fellowships is important, but not enough. You need to invest personal time in seeking God so you can get to know Him for yourself by yourself. This makes the corporate church experience richer and the body of Christ stronger, when we know Jesus personally. It is the most beautiful thing in the world when the church is united around Jesus as the center and without any other agenda. Therein Yahweh commands the blessing! (Psalms 133:1)

I started to invest my weekly stipends on the road touring with the choir on buying Christian books about real-life experiences written by Jesus followers that would be relatable and help build me up. I read from people like Billy Graham, Bishop T.D Jakes, Joel Osteen, Joseph Prince, Brother Lawrence, John Bevere, Joyce Meyer, John Ortberg etc. I started to read the Bible and pray with a new passion, like I had been born again, again. We need more people in the church to get born again, again. We need a church on fire! A lit up church! I have realized on my journey that even though reading books takes you into other people's experiences and helps you grow your Christian perspective, reading books is not enough. Obedience and submission to God's Spirit leading you is what really changes you. Following God's uncomfortable, inconvenient instructions will teach you a lot more than a 500-page best seller book on effective Christian ministry ever could. In fact, your obedience to God in the unknown will help you relate to the stories in the books you read and make the author's own stories play out in yours. You will gain some life-changing insight and spiritual guidance by reading this book. I hope you do. But the real transformation will happen in your life when you allow God to take you on your own journey of awakening. When you get on that narrow, inconvenient, confusing, uncomfortable and painful path God calls you on in obedience and surrender, you will start to see God as you've never seen Him before.

"You need to invest personal time in seeking God so you can get to know Him for yourself by yourself."

On the narrow path, God will reveal all the spiritual strongholds and strangleholds that were invited into your life as a result of your lifestyle choices. God will shine a bright light in you and reveal the darkness, plus help you drive it out, so that His light can shine through you brightly. The transformed life is an exchanged life. Where darkness lived, the light of Jesus takes center stage and shines bright through us. God is often gentle when He reveals us to ourselves. Sometimes He does it in third person, so it appears as if He was talking about someone else. Every time you dream about someone in your life, whatever is happening in the dream most of the time is a parable reference to your own character. So do not be in a hurry to tell the third person about how you saw them in your dream and how you need to pray for them. Sometimes it's about them, but most of the time, God uses other people we know to show us something about ourselves. Being the light of the world is not about quoting scripture or about good behavior; those are just parts of it. Being a light starts on the inside, when God takes the place of whatever you were drunk on before and replaces it with His light so that what comes out of us is light. It is the closest experience to Heaven on earth, because that is the life of Heaven residing inside of you and touching the world through you. If we do not allow this to happen, we are like actors who go through the motions of ministry but never experience the power of the Holy Spirit.

> *"You are the light of the world. A town built on a hill cannot be hidden. Neither do people light a lamp and put it under a bowl. Instead, they put it on its stand, and it gives light to everyone in the house. In the same way, let your light shine before others, that they may see your good deeds and glorify your Father in heaven.*

> **(Matthew 5:14-16)**

Being the light of the world is not about perfection. If it was, no human on earth would meet the standard. I'm not there yet, still have questions and struggles, but I'm on the right path. I do not need to pretend to have it all together. I do not need to act, I'm a work in progress and I am daily being transformed even as the eternal part of me has already been perfected by the finished work of the cross. It is in realizing my frailty and weakness that God's strength works through me even more strongly. We are channels, conduits of light. God's light does not come from us. It comes through us. If we are mastered by addictions, we hinder the flow of light through us. We may talk light, but darkness is what resides in and comes out, so we are ineffective for the Kingdom. Jesus wants to turn your dark places into light.

Redemption is a lifelong journey, so you must commit to it for the long haul. Do not delay another minute to start the uncomfortable yet inevitable journey of dying so you may indeed live. If you really want to be all that God created you to be, you must deal with the inconvenience of it. I have had the most beautiful, revealing journey with the Holy Spirit, but things just keep getting revealed when the right circumstances are presented. Sometimes anger, other times fear, sometimes doubt and insecurity and selfish desires. But they do not control me anymore. Jesus has a hold on me, even though these things keep rearing their heads. Sin will always keep raising its head. It is our job to keep putting that head in its place. Like Joyce Meyer puts it, *"You cannot stop birds from flying over your head, but you can stop them from building a nest on your head."*

Chapter 3

Deliverance

Don't you realize that your bodies are actually parts of Christ? Should a man take his body, which is part of Christ, and join it to a prostitute? Never! And don't you realize that if a man joins himself to a prostitute, he becomes one body with her? For the Scriptures say, "The two are united into one." But the person who is joined to the Lord is one spirit with him. Run from sexual sin! No other sin so clearly affects the body as this one does. For sexual immorality is a sin against your own body. Don't you realize that your body is the temple of the Holy Spirit, who lives in you and was given to you by God? You do not belong to yourself, for God bought you with a high price. So you must honor God with your body.

(1 Corinthians 6:15-20)

I t is God's desire that believers would be free from being dominated by anything other than the Spirit of Almighty God Himself. After all, we are God's temple. God wants that we will make our lives a habitation for His presence. It is what makes us effective representatives of the Kingdom. To be dominated by something that we cannot live without that is not the presence of the Spirit of Almighty God in our lives is to be under the influence of another kingdom. We are addicted. Addictions are usually sustained by the presence of familiar spirits. These are demonic spirits that prompt or influence certain behavior in a person. These spirits are familiar with our history and our weaknesses. We become one with them when we engage in deliberate sinful practices. They know the areas where we are weakest and will always suggest those areas. The patterns of familiar spirits are very predictable. When one starts to have sex outside marriage - fornication or practice masturbation or pornography, these spirits are invited to assume residence in that individual. Their job is to make you feel powerless against the addiction, while continually suggesting it and make you feel like you cannot overcome it. Part of you does not like the addiction, is embarrassed about it, wants to end it, but the flesh is incapable of victory against spiritual forces without the superior Spirit of Christ. You remember that scripture; *"The spirit is willing, but the flesh is weak"* **(Matthew 26:41)**

Make no mistake, held up in addictions, you have opened yourself up to the demonic. This is why it is impossible for God to use us for His purposes in a great way when we are still held up in these practices. These demonic spirits are against the spirit of Christ. They are literally the antichrist at work in us. Darkness and light do not work together.

There are people who are actively involved in ministry who are still held captive in the things that keep one bound and limited. They are gifted people, talented and consistent and sincere, but their spiritual impact is continually being undermined by the presence of familiar spirits. This is what creates the social club syndrome in the church, where we celebrate talent and skill and miss the presence of God.

Do not mistake someone's talent and giftedness for the anointing of the Holy Spirit. If you are a person that wants to fulfill your God-given destiny and not just go through the motions of church, you are going to have to confront these things in your life. If not, God Himself will confront you. God often deals with us privately, convicting us, nudging us, hoping we will respond. God speaks in a whisper to get our attention on a particular area in our lives. If we do not hear, He speaks louder. If we still do not, He gets louder, and if we still do not, bricks are thrown at us to get our attention. God will go to great lengths to get our attentions to help us fulfill our destiny.

Courage to overcome

Many people do not change because they reject God's offer of help. They want a fix, but they want it their way, with minimal inconvenience and discomfort. They want to save face. God just take it away from me they sincerely cry. I did that for a long time. Spiritual transformation doesn't work like that. It takes courage to be truly free. Some people run away from turning points when God has pulled a drastic move on them that exposes them, embarrasses them and calls them to change. I was consistently committed to performing my ministry work with excellence, but was undermined in my spiritual effectiveness because of the presence of familiar ungodly spirits that I had given residence to because of masturbation and pornography in my life. It is better to face the humiliation of a turning point that exposes you, but delivers and transforms you, than run away, explain yourself away, and continue to put on a bold front that is empty and powerless and keeps you impotent for the Kingdom all your life. To derive confidence from the approval you get from people for your giftedness and performance does not serve the Kingdom. It only serves you. God likes to shatter the thing we have built confidence out of so that our confidence can come from the true source - God Himself.

When God cornered me at my turning point, I would have run away, but I would have never changed and grown. God has the right people to corner you. People who truly love Him and have been challenged and changed themselves. They do not act from condemnation but compassion. God will corner you, so He brings deliverance in your life and so you can do more together. Like I mentioned earlier, God got my attention by removing a well-earned promotion from me. It was well earned speaking in human terms. I had built myself a reputation as a hard worker, but I had not built a reputation with the God who sees in secret as one who does their best to honor Him. That experience was absolutely humbling, but it was the best thing that could happen to me at that time. It got me on a journey of self-reflection, to cease to depend on my gifts or work reputation, but completely depend on the gift giver, on God Himself for my reputation. This was my turning point following Jesus. I had been born again, again. I started to feel a peace and excitement for the future like I had only experienced when I first gave my heart to Jesus. I started to understand what ministry looks like from God's point of view.

You see, like I said earlier, I grew up embarrassed about my earthly father and was always looking for something to hold on to that gave me a sense of identity. I realized I had found my identity as an adult in my performance in my ministry work. It was time to find my true identity in that which I would not lose, in my Heavenly Father! In the scripture I shared at the start of this section, Paul says that one who unites himself with a prostitute becomes one with her. Now, you may say, no, I have not slept with a prostitute. But did you know that looking at pornographic images is prostitution? Masturbating over an image in your mind is fornication and prostitution too. You are giving yourself over to all these images you look at and inviting a union with familiar spirits. You are becoming one with demonic spirits. Is that frightening? I hope it is! It is also true because I have seen God take me back into those scenarios and deliver me. I wish I could frighten enough people who are caught up in these things to make the shift ASAP. The church needs you. God needs you. Your body is a temple of the Holy Spirit. Your impact on the body of Christ depends on your willingness to make the shift or allow the shift to take place and not run away when the heat is turned up.

When God started to deal with me, it caused me to confront things in my life I had never confronted before. Pride and fear ruled my life and I did not even know it. I justified myself. I was controlling and impatient with people. I was deeply insecure and manipulative. I was a complete chicken too, but you could not tell because I put on a bold front. I was a fake and I could see it, wanted to do something about it, but did not know how. I prayed to God to remove it from me, repented a million times, but nothing changed. It was only until God took something that took His place in my life, like a performance-related promotion, that I defined myself by that it hit home. I have seen God remove things from me since. I have experienced financial losses, relationship failures, and seen familiar spirits leave in spiritual deliverance and felt the freedom of Jesus. I wish I could tell you that you will be instantly delivered as some would like. There is instant healing, but there is a process to being delivered. A process that goes on for a long time and you must stay the course with God for His deliverance to continue in your life. The goal ultimately is to cultivate intimacy with Jesus. We are daily being delivered as Jesus wins us over to Himself. The goal is to give Jesus precedence over your life in areas you had given precedence to other controlling spirits through addictions. You must have the courage to confront, to own up, to face embarrassment, even humiliation, but whatever it takes, you must be free so that you can walk in God's purposes for you. Your purpose in God must mean more to you than saving face if you are going to become the person God created you to be.

**"Christianity is a takeover movement, and it is for
a complete takeover."**

Freedom

It is for freedom that Christ has set us free. Stand firm, then, and do not let yourselves be burdened again by a yoke of slavery.

(Galatians 5:1)

When I let go of the animosity, hatred, shame and embarrassment I felt toward my earthly father, I felt a big weight lift off of me. I felt freedom! This was when I started to understand what it means to be a slave. Many people hold on to past hurts like there is a prize for it. I know what it's like to hold on to past hurt like it's some kind of entitlement prize. This only hurts you and makes you miserable. I was miserably depressed for a long time and had no idea why. I couldn't put a finger on it. But when I started to get honest with my dad and confront all the shame and embarrassment I held toward him that I was hiding on the inside, I started to experience freedom I had never experienced before. Overcoming depression was not just related to my dad. It was a whole lot of other issues, fears, worries, insecurities in my life that had nothing to do with my dad. Sometimes it is easy to blame someone else as the cause of all your problems, but looking at the man in the mirror always helps us see who the real source of our troubles is. I may have used my dad as a scapegoat, but I was a slave of my own making and I did not even know it. Besides, way after my dad passed and our relationship was healed, I have still found myself miserable over things I used to blame him for. I still have to continually check that I am not blaming someone else, even blaming God for things I have held on to and need to own up to that seek to undermine my effectiveness for the Kingdom.

You can rebuke the devil all you want, go to prayer and deliverance meetings all you want, even seek out a man of God to lay hands on you. None of that will work and the problem is not with your church or your pastor or your work mates or your spouse. The problem is you are still holding on to things you should let go of. You have enslaved yourself and you don't know it. I must say this is the problem with many people in the church. This was my problem for a long time till I woke up. Many people are expecting their pastor or church leader or spouse or Jesus to deliver them from something even Jesus wants them to let go of. Christianity is a takeover movement, but God won't force His will on us. We let go of who we were, so that we allow who we are meant to be and called to be to occupy the space of who we used to be. It is a process that takes a commitment of a lifetime. Paul explains the path to deliverance and freedom from spiritual slavery in the most straightforward, simple yet compelling way I have witnessed in the book of Ephesians.

> So I tell you this, and insist on it in the Lord, that you must no longer live as the Gentiles do, in the futility of their thinking. They are darkened in their understanding and separated from the life of God because of the ignorance that is in them due to the hardening of their hearts. Having lost all sensitivity, they have given themselves over to sensuality so as to indulge in every kind of impurity, and they are full of greed. That, however, is not the way of life you learned when you heard about Christ and were

taught in him in accordance with the truth that is in Jesus. You were taught, with regard to your former way of life, to put off your old self, which is being corrupted by its deceitful desires; to be made new in the attitude of your minds; and to put on the new self, created to be like God in true righteousness and holiness. Therefore each of you must put off falsehood and speak truthfully to your neighbor, for we are all members of one body. "In your anger, do not sin": Do not let the sun go down while you are still angry, and do not give the devil a foothold. Anyone who has been stealing must steal no longer, but must work, doing something useful with their own hands, that they may have something to share with those in need. Do not let any unwholesome talk come out of your mouths, but only what is helpful for building others up according to their needs, that it may benefit those who listen. And do not grieve the Holy Spirit of God, with whom you were sealed for the day of redemption. Get rid of all bitterness, rage and anger, brawling and slander, along with every form of malice. Be kind and compassionate to one another, forgiving each other, just as in Christ God forgave you.

(Ephesians 4:17–32)

This portion of scripture clearly stipulates our responsibility in the journey of deliverance and freedom. Holding on to past hurts can harden our hearts. I used to wonder why many of my relationships with girls were short-lived and did not work out. I always blamed the other person as being shallow or spiritually immature or as not being genuine until I started to look inside myself and realize my own heart was hardened and that made me difficult to relate with because I was emotionally disconnected, plus I was insecure and controlling, wanting things my way, not looking at things from the other persons point of view. When I got hurt because I felt rejected by someone, I held a grudge and it was only a matter of time till I would express it and in a most negative way, which would destroy a relationship that was working out for me.

I have quit on some relationships because of my own instability and indecisiveness, plus the desire for perfection. Some relationships have quit on me and broke my heart. Perfectionism, far from revealing how good we are, often reveals how disconnected from reality we are. I looked at everything logically and love is not logical a lot of the time. True love is risky and vulnerable, not controlling! God so loved the world. He risked dying on the cross for us before we indicated we would love Him back. God did not wait to hear that we had decided to change our ways. He went all in regardless of what our response would be.

Paul says to put off, to let go of and this should be a point of revelation for someone reading this who has been struggling. Many of the things you are asking God to free you from, things you are even frustrated that He is not delivering you from despite your genuine plea for help, He is expecting you to let go of.

If you have been lying, let go of it, Paul says. Oh yeah! That simple? Yes!

From my own experience, you just have to stop fighting it and let go. The more we try to fight sin, the stronger it gets a grip on us. We were never meant to fight in our own strength, but to constantly bring it and ourselves to the superior victorious presence of Jesus Christ. Accepting yourself and honestly acknowledging your weaknesses and shortcomings because God accepts you even though He knows everything about you is one of life's most liberating things. You have to start practicing being truthful little by little. You do not let go of what you have been held in for years overnight. There is no such thing as overnight transformation from a life of sin. Deliverance from slavery happens in increments as we stay the process. The day we got saved started a process. You can take a man from the village, but it takes a while to take the village out of the man. As Paul says;

"We are daily being saved."

(2 Corinthians 4:16)

Self-rejection

I would like to talk about an area I have had to address in my life. An area that grew because of the escapist in me wanting to be part of another family. I did not realize then, as I know now, that running away from my family truth, no matter what my dad was like, was running away from myself. It was self-rejection. Most pretense and falsehood arises from self-rejection. You do not think you have it in you, so you pretend to be what you are not to have a better chance at being accepted. Self-rejection is present in people who try very hard to impress and keep up appearances and I know this because I did that.

I used to lie a lot, sugarcoat a lot or exaggerate a lot, do more than was required to make myself or things look better than they were and the reason was to make people like me or just to paint a more favorable look of things. Like I said before, I would have done anything as a child to be part of another family, to have a different earthly father to the one I had. So to make people think better of me than I thought they would, I lied about my family background, lied about my grades, lied about the schools I went to, lied about the community I lived in. I wanted people to think me better off than I really was. I'm a different man now, thank God, even though I'm still learning and growing, I know who I am and whose I am. I have been redeemed!

I found out that you can only keep up impressions long enough. Eventually, your truth will come out. Someone who knew you from the past will show up or your own words will not add up. An old friend will show up and call you by that name you no longer want to associate yourself with and you will want to disappear, not because you are an undercover agent, but a pretender. It's a tough life trying to be who you are not. I wish I could say that you overcome this as soon as you receive Jesus, but no. As you can see, it has been a journey, one that I continue on every day. Oh, but what freedom I have found in finally accepting my history. In knowing my past, my family background greatly contributed to who I became, but it doesn't define who I'm called to be in Christ. I found freedom in accepting and embracing my history, and everyone who is some kind of escapist as I was will find freedom in letting go of the illusion of controlling how people see you. You will find that many people don't even care. They are too concerned about themselves and their own issues to mind you. They just want to know what you have to offer and holding on to falsehood, trying to keep up impressions will hinder the quality of what you have to offer because the original you is far superior to the pretend you.

Keeping up a false appearance to impress others diminishes your quality greatly. It is better to be honest about your limitations and shortcomings. Your terrible history is far better than a fake story. People cut you more slack when you are genuine, but fail to live up to certain expectations. But people can be unforgiving if you have given them the impression you are better than you actually present yourself to be. They will expect more and be disappointed, plus you will always be disappointed in yourself too trying to be what you are not, plus deep inside, you hate yourself, even though you will deflect that onto others and accuse others of hating you. Self-rejection always leads to a projection of the same on other people, so does self-love. You will think everyone that says no to you had rejected you when in actual fact, they had other reasons. Self-rejection creates a victim mentality in you. You think the world is against you. I mentioned earlier how I liked to start fights, most of which I lost. I was always trying to prove something; that I was important and someone needed to know it and acknowledge it. God knows it. He says it to me, "You are important, son" I am learning that it is enough what God says about me.

Most of the time that I tried to prove myself, there was nothing to prove. This carried on into my adulthood and turned into a spirit of competition and comparison. When I started to lead the songs in the church services, I was trying to lead worship better than someone else or preach better than someone else, not realizing we are one big family and we are all in this together for the glory of our Heavenly father no matter who does what as long as we all do our best. When someone did better than me, I felt inferior. When I appeared better than someone, I felt superior even when no one was keeping score. The flip side of that is never appreciating what I did even when others did. I always felt like I did not do too well, that my effort needed improvement. Even when I gave my best and everyone applauded, there was still an inner feeling that just did not want to accept that I really did well or could do well. I did not easily receive compliments. Self-rejection sucks!

Self-rejection always leads to a projection of the same on other people, so does self-love.

Falsehood is a demonic spirit that seeks to undermine your true identity in Christ. The enemy knows our past and works 24/7 to try and make our past our reality so that we do not experience our future in Christ. If you have been practicing falsehood to keep up impressions for whatever reason, know that it will greatly undermine your purpose in Christ. Time to put it off, to let it go. Allow God to back you up and be your reputation when you feel like you don't have it in you. God wants to be our strength. The devil is called a masquerader, an imposter, a fake, a liar from the beginning and the father of all lairs and he is desperately looking for company, but he doesn't deserve yours or mine. We are children of the most high God. Let God be your strength and cover when you feel like you do not have it in you.

> But he said to me, "My grace is sufficient for you, for my power is made perfect in weakness." Therefore I will boast all the more gladly about my weaknesses, so that Christ's power may rest on me. That is why, for Christ's sake, I delight in weaknesses, in insults, in hardships, in persecutions, in difficulties. For when I am weak, then I am strong.

(2 Corinthians 12:9-10)

True deliverance is happening, when we are continually learning to lean on God's strength, and less on ourselves. It is happening when our confidence is built on Christ even when we feel inadequate and afraid, yet we keep doing what God has called us to do in fear and weakness, leaning on divine strength. We are being emptied of who we were as we become who we are meant to be. God does not just want to give us strength. He wants to be our strength.

Chapter 4

Angry or Something?

Many people are angry and they do not know why they are so angry. I was such a one. I was angry at my earthly father, angry at myself, angry at the world, just angry about everything. Some folks boast of having a short fuse like there is a prize for it. In fact, some people have even accepted their short temper as who they are. They have formed an identity around it, and expect people to respect them for it. The truth is a short fuse is not a fruit of the holy spirit. It is nothing to boast about. It is a liability, not an asset, and hinders God's purposes in many people's lives.

> *A fool shows his annoyance at once, but a prudent man overlooks an insult.*
>
> **(Proverbs 12:16)**

I discovered my own anger came from not accepting who I was. I always wanted to be someone else, pretending to be that person, lying to appear like that person I wanted to be, always falling short and frustrated it did not magically work. I was angry at who I really was, hated myself but did not even know why I was angry. For a long time, I blamed my dad for it. I thought to myself if only my dad had been like other responsible dads. Then I blamed myself for not being like other guys. Comparison is a passion and confidence killer.

Then you will know the truth, and the truth will set you free."

(John 8:32)

The truth hurts, but it sets people free. Many people would rather embrace a comforting lie than an uncomfortable truth. This is the leading cause of superficiality in the church and in the world. Superficialness stifles fellowship in the church, fans the flames of gossip and quenches the power of the Holy Spirit in the church who operates where there is truth and transparency.

I want to talk about American politics and current affairs a little. When Donald Trump won the presidency of the United States of America in 2016, there are those who responded with surprise, others with relief saying, "Thank God!" Others with excitement and celebration, then there were those who responded with furious anger. The mainstream media was up in arms. The Democrats were up in arms. Half of America was upset. It was perhaps one of the presidential election victories in American history that has drawn the most extreme reactions on both ends. There were angry outbursts, expressions of hate for the man and for those who supported him. Some even refused his known supporters' restaurant services. If you didn't check for yourself, you would have thought Trump some kind of evil sorcerer. Marriages got broken, families separated, friendships ended and not in nice ways. Many people in America and around the world were angry, and not in reasonable ways, and they all blamed it on this one man - Trump. I thought to myself, how can one person have so much control over so many people's emotions so as to cause them to lose their minds, to walk away from family and from marriages and friendships, that cannot be. If you had an objective view of Trump, they thought you racist. Now, I'm a black man who has suffered some effects of racism, but I know racism is not a black and white thing. It is a human thing. Some of the most racist people I know in this world try their best to act the nicest in public. They are politically correct. Could it be that Trump only acted as a catalyst to awaken and bring to light un-confronted, underlying bitter personal realities? Could it be that the way he projected himself and his weaknesses reminded many of their own? Could it be that he exposed the superficiality that was already in place in political correctness with his unfiltered, carefree tough talk?

Trump is not perfect. He has issues as everyone does. He could hold back on what he says sometimes, but so could everyone. The thing is, Trump was not called racist until he ran for president. People celebrated his tough stance on the reality show "The Apprentice" and even loved his two famous words; "You're fired!" I mean, I have watched YouTube videos of the very people, some black influencers who called him racist as a president who encouraged him to run for president long before he ever did. What changed?

Could it be that many who thought Trump was one of them felt abandoned when Trump run on a conservative ticket and on conservative policies? Many of us have not been tested at high levels of leadership, but we might not even like ourselves and what comes out if we were placed in the most powerful position on planet earth. Trump has had marriage failures, relationship failures, business failures, bankruptcy and, in equal measure, business successes to the point he did not take a salary as president. This one man, in my opinion, was mischaracterized and misrepresented by mainstream, agenda-driven media on purpose to show him to the world in a certain light with the intention to discredit everything he did.

I mean, the guy killed a known terrorist who was responsible for the death of American soldiers, but the media celebrated the terrorist while presenting Trump as a xenophobic hater. I'll tell you why. They were offended. They were angry at Trump and thought it was their duty to get rid of him at any cost, even if it meant making a known terrorist look better than him. But, was the problem Trump or was he just a tool of exposure?

Here is the thing; If an outside party I have only recently come to know about can cause such an uprooting in my family to the point of separation of siblings, parents, marriages, was it the outside party's fault, or was it that there was some underlying weakness in my family not yet acknowledged that was waiting like a ticking time bomb to go off. Like one anonymous writer said;

"Ships don't sink because of the water around them; ships sink because of the water that gets in them."

If we do not deal with our inner selves, Trump will disappear and it's just a matter of time and someone else or something else will show up and cause angry division. The glue of relationships is not an outside force. It is an inside disposition. We are either loyal, committed, emotionally healthy people, or we are not. A government has no power to fix the inner lives of people, the people who run the government need a fix too themselves. Only the Church of Jesus Christ has the mandate to bring healing to the nations in the name of Jesus.

Sometimes we are angry with others because we see ourselves in them, and what they portray reveals unhealed aspects of ourselves. People are a mirror. In fact, all of humanity is a mirror. What we see in others is in us. What we do not see in others lacks in us. When you are wounded, you are more likely to notice other wounded people. When you are healed or being healed, you are more likely to notice healing in others. Sometimes it may appear that the most critical person among us is the most knowledgeable and upright, but I have found that to be far from the truth. Sometimes the most critical of us is the most wounded and unhealed of us. Looking at my own life, the more healing I have found for my wounds, the more compassion I have developed for those I notice who are wounded in places I used to be wounded. Also, the more critical I have been of others, the more I have seen what I criticized in them in me.

Sometimes we are angry at others because we see our own deficiency in them. We are helpless to do anything about it, so we naturally blame the one who triggered us. Perhaps Trump has simply highlighted the blame-shifting where people blame all outside sources for their distress but never look in the mirror to say. Perhaps I need to own up and grow some inner stamina to withstand the sometimes cruel realities of the world. We struggle to accept our condition because we think we should be in a better position and someone else should be held responsible for us being the way we are.

We are each responsible for our reactions and responses to people and things in life. Our reactions often do not reveal the person we react to. They reveal us. The best response to anger is ownership. Looking inside for what triggers our anger will bring healing. But continually blaming someone else will leave us in a perpetual state of woundedness for the things Jesus came to deliver us from. Jesus cannot deliver you from what you blame someone else for. It's only a matter of time and there will always be someone else to trigger you if you do not address it from inside. Anger makes people unreasonable. It blinds you from seeing which way is up. Trump had only been president for a year at the end of 2017, but to many people, he was responsible for America's problems from 1945. Meanwhile, those who had actually been in government for decades and would be the ones to be held responsible are not. Why? Because they are politically correct, speak the establishment, status quo language and haven't offended the media as to cause anger.

For a long time, I blamed my dad and everyone for how I reacted or acted until I came to the revelation, Where is my power? What is my responsibility? My father, the man I blamed, did not get any proper guidance himself. He grew up by accident too, in a dysfunctional family. In fact, his family had way more dysfunctional issues in that he was born in a polygamous family. His father had many wives and children, plus the massive dysfunction that comes with it.

When I started to look at my dad as a victim too, I started to have more compassion for him and for myself and started directing my anger at the real enemy. I was my own enemy for not dealing with my issues the right way. We have an outside enemy called Lucifer, a.k.a the devil whose only plan is to steal, kill and destroy. When we do not address our dysfunctional issues the right way from the inside, we give the devil control over us. The devil wants nothing but for us to stay in a place of dysfunction because he knows we will be self-destructive and not be able to fulfill our Heavenly purpose that way. You see, we give to others what abides in us. If Jesus and His miracle-working power through the Holy Spirit abides in us, that is what we give off to the world. If we function on dysfunction, that is what we give off to the world. The devil wants nothing more than to have humans operating out of dysfunction while not taking responsibility.

I came to realize I had spent my life blaming someone for my problems. Someone who did not know any better himself. We were both victims. The devil is a liar and the perpetrator of all deflection in order to avoid addressing the heart of the matter. The devil operates in chaos and unreasonableness that deflects from truthfully handling situations. He thrives on the blame game, because that way, nothing changes. My dad needed help that he did not receive growing up, just like

I did. He passed on what he received. My father needed to be Fathered just like I did. You will always blame someone else for your issues and those issues will remain until you wake up and name the issue for what it is, plus your responsibility in it. I know that I won't ever be perfect in this human frame, but when I finally meet my pretty girl and get married and have some kids, I do not want to pass on the dysfunction I inherited from my dad. I want to pass on a legacy of Jesus and His healing, liberating, miracle-working power along with my human DNA.

Do not be wise in your own eyes; fear the Lord and shun evil. This will bring health to your body and nourishment to your bones.

(Proverbs 3:5-6)

One self-destructive thing people tend to do is justify their dysfunction by coming up with the most appropriate and clever, scientific excuse to allow oneself to continue in dysfunction Jesus died to set humanity free from. We have seen this kind of reasoning gaining traction over the last 50 years in America, Europe, in fact, much of the western world. This is just the way I am. It is how God made me, people reason. Don't be a hater, be tolerant, some angrily demand. The biblical definition of tolerance is bearing with one another's weaknesses. It is not supporting a dysfunction one was born to overcome, but has chosen to settle in and justify. No matter how good you dress a pig, it will always be a pig. You can costume it with the most expensive and flamboyant apparel and even give it another name, but inside that pretty and expensive costume, it is still very much a pig and will always be a pig with all its pig proclivities. This is what people who push agendas do. There is a difference between weakness and dysfunction. Dysfunction can be corrected and healed. Weakness, however, is a part of human nature. It is the mistakes we make in judgment, the things we mishandle and break, the miscalculations we make that can have catastrophic implications, we all fall short. The Bible says,

For all have sinned and fall short of the glory of God, and all are justified freely by his grace through the redemption that came by Christ Jesus.

(Romans 3:23-24)

You notice the Bible says we are **justified through the redemption that came by Christ Jesus**. True Jesus followers do not show tolerance by supporting the very agendas He died to **redeem** humanity from. True Jesus followers allow the **redemptive**, life-saving presence of Christ to invade hearts and relationships with the truth that sets men free. The truth is not what one thinks. Truth is not a scientific opinion on a matter. There is no such thing as your own truth. There is THE STANDARD OF TRUTH in the Bible, in the person of Jesus Christ. Everything else comes from the evil one whose only plan is to steal, kill and destroy humanity. All things find their existence from Christ Jesus.

Through Him, all things were made; and without Him, nothing was made that has been made.

(John 1:3)

Science would not exist without Christ, who was with God in the beginning and created all things. Science finds its raw materials from God's creation. Without God's creation, there would be no science. Without God, there is nothing that is anything because nothing would exist without God.

Jesus would not call supporting dysfunctional agenda tolerance, but being an accomplice to the enemy's plan against humanity.

> But whoever causes one of these little ones who believe in Me to stumble and sin (by leading them away from My teaching), it would be better for him to have a heavy millstone (as large as one turned by a donkey) hung around his neck and to be drowned in the depth of the sea.

(Matthew 18:6)

Some of the enemy's deception is, we are the only ones struggling with this, the only ones wounded in this area. We must be some kind of weirdos. It is not true! Everyone else is as human as we are, dealing with something humans deal with just as we are. What you say to yourself can be very self-destructive. We need to continually be open to what God says about us. God is honest, says it as it is. God is not afraid to offend you in order to help you. We need friends who mean us well, who are honest with us. It is better to have an enemy who tells you the truth they see about your issues than so-called friends who tell you all the good for nothing stuff about yourself that boosts your ego. The Bible says.

> Where there is no counsel, the people fall; But in a multitude of counselors, there is safety.

(Proverbs 11:14)

Do not wait to deal with dysfunction in your life, to acknowledge it for what it is no matter what it is, small or big. God waits for us to be honest about our situation before He brings Heaven's answers to our situations. Justifying our situations only breaks God's heart. Spiritual growth and transformation is simply a change of mind. It is getting God's mind and counsel about you and about life.

The more we get God's mind about us and about others, the more healing we will experience and peace we will have, the less anger we will express, the less triggered we will be and the more productive we will be. We will change the world!

> As a father has compassion on his children, so the Lord has compassion on those who fear Him; for He knows how we are formed, He remembers that we are dust. The life of mortals is like grass, they flourish like a flower of the field; the wind blows over it and it is gone, and in its place remembers it no more. but from everlasting to everlasting the Lord's love is with those who fear Him, and His righteousness with their children's children – with those who keep His covenant and remember to obey His precepts.

(Psalms 103:13-18)

Before Trump won the 2016 election, God said to me he was going to win it. I did not know how. It did not look likely from the polls. But what God says always goes. The thing about God is He never gives people what they want. He gives us what we need. Perhaps President Trump and the anger that has been directed at him, plus revealed in many people and families was God's way of shaking up the status quo, of challenging the superficiality of political correctness many people have accepted as normal. We all hate it when what we have accepted and justified as truth is completely challenged to its root. Trump is a complete opposite of Obama in personality and policy priorities. Some church people called Trump the antichrist but far from it. I was excited when Obama was elected in 2008. It was a testament of how far America had come. But, on the night Obama was inaugurated, I had a dream that a monument to the antichrist was being set up. Did not understand what that meant at the time, but when I later looked at his policy priorities that were agenda-driven, I understood the dream.

Trump has had witches cast spells on him and witches would not try to cast out an anti-Christ because they are anti-Christ themselves. He had constantly bad publicity from people who unreasonably hated him, but prevailed even through an impeachment. I think that even with the outcome of the recent US 2020 election that had many reports of glitches, fraud and irregularities that are said to have influenced the outcome in some states, God is still using Trump as a tool and his purpose in the shaking of the status quo is not finished. The lawsuits about election fraud did not gain traction even with the evidence presented, so we do not know fully and cannot confirm what happened legally, but I did have several dreams about the election irregularities. I think that everything is going just as it is supposed to because God is not finished with His plans for America. If Trump were not a threat to agenda's nobody would not fight him as they have. The establishment has pulled every card they possibly can on this one man. The truth always comes out, it cannot stay hidden forever, so it will come out one day for all to truly see. The wrath of man does not bring about God's righteousness. (James 1:20)

Righteous anger...

There is a different kind of anger that we must have or else we have become accomplices to evil. We must be angry at true injustice where people are denied their God-given rights. You notice I say, "God-given rights." Some of the rights people push for are not God-given. They are rebellious choices against God's creation order. They are deceptive demands like Eve in the garden choosing to listen to the voice of the serpent because she thought it would bring her and her husband into a whole new world of knowledge. It did, but it also destroyed them forever. Clamoring for justice for selfish life choices away from God's plan for humanity only makes the world worse. It is what I call perverted justice.

Let me share some examples of righteous anger; Christ, when He was angry that they had turned the temple of God into a den of thieves, He gave the traders a whipping. Moses when he broke all ten commandments at once when he found Israel dancing around a golden calf on his way down the mountain from receiving God's commandments for Israel. Samuel when he noticed Saul did not fully follow all of God's commands as given to him. Saul followed some of God's instructions, but did not fully observe everything God said to him. Martin Luther King Jr. was championing the civil rights movements pressing for life, liberty and justice for all, not just some Americans. We should be angry at things that are upside down enough to do something about setting them right side up. Some people today use Martin Luther King Jr in their fights for agendas that he never had anything to do with or would support if he were here today. His movement was simply upright justice, God-given rights, not selfish, empty demands!

When we see something that directly stands against the will of God and the written word in the Bible, we should be angry. However, the Bible says in your anger, do not sin. Righteous anger always leads us to righteous actions that are directed at correcting the evil we see in society and in our own lives.

Then there's ignorant, selfish anger like Jonah, not happy that God did not destroy the city of Nineveh; or Peter's ignorant anger cutting the ear of one of the men who came to arrest Jesus. When Jesus placed the man's ear back on, Peter was confused, he was angry, he did not understand Jesus. He thought he was helping Jesus by cutting an ear and now Jesus was fixing the enemy? Peter went on to deny Jesus three times because he could no longer understand this man he had followed for over three years. Can you identify with Peter or Jonah? I do! God knows how many times I have been ignorantly, and stupidly angry thinking I was serving God's purpose.

You will get angry trying to understand everything God does or allows. A lot of what God does and allows, we will understand in hindsight. Instead of flying off the handle, ruining everything that is already going well for you because of the one thing you do not like or understand, it is better to relax, take a chill pill, you will have a better reaction and understanding of something when you make slow down, relax your life principle. I wish this was easy. I'm learning every day.

The devil likes people reacting in anger to anything that offends them or anything they don't understand and cannot control. He knows anger will blind you to the good things of life. It will make you ruin even the good things that you already have going for you. The devil is a liar!

Paul says do not give the devil a foothold. Anger is a foothold that gives the devil room to unleash destruction on our lives. He destroys relationships, steals opportunities and takes lives riding on the angry actions people take. Anger will lead you down a self-destructive path even though you may think it is affecting those you are angry at. God redeems our lives by exposing us to the very things that hurt us and anger us, things that we fear, things we hate and run away from because they traumatized us deeply. God loves to take us into the messy situations that traumatized us, but this time so we get to face them with Him and see them from His perspective. God allows circumstances that reveal us to ourselves, that bring to light what is hidden in the darkness. It's the path of healing, the path of redemption. I wish it was any different, but until you are willing to go with God into the pain, the hurt, the anger deep inside, you forfeit the healing and the freedom that comes with it. Do not rebuke the devil when you are exposed to what hurt you. God wants to walk with you through the trauma, so you see the situation from His point of view and are completely set free from its power over you.

Many people say that what you go through makes you and wisdom comes with age and experience, but I have discovered that is not true. Everyone will go through a fair share of trouble and trouble will reveal what is already in the heart. Trouble reveals our world view. It reveals our hearts, our faults. You can respond by changing or by blaming someone else for what is revealed. When our hearts are revealed, it is better to face up and grow up or we will stay in denial and become stunted in our growth. You can be old and foolish. You can be young and wise. It all depends on how you respond to God and the life He offers. God said this to me; *"Circumstances do not make you. They reveal you. What makes you is how you respond to the life God offers you."*

I found this to be one of the most sobering statements I ever heard in my life. It awakened me from slumber, from blaming my earthly father or other people for my own poor choices and responses and outbursts of anger. When I started to own up, I started to grow up. When I started to work on owning my anger, I started to build a more stable, emotionally happy and peaceful life. The fruit of the Spirit is not given to us as an answer to prayer. The fruit of the Spirit grows like fruit grows in the garden from seed form to a full-grown, fruit-bearing plant. This is a scientific, organic process, and the Spiritual process is organic too.

When a seed is planted, it endures dark, difficult days before it sprouts to life as it stretches towards the sun. The soil elements and the darkness surrounding it reveal the quality of the seed. It's the same with us. In order for us to grow and be fruitful, we must be planted in good soil with darkness surrounding us so that, like God's seed, we are revealed, overcome and stretch towards the SON. I have spoken about anger towards people and life, but there are a lot of people who are angry at God. I know I have been time and again.

Has God ever said something to you He was going to do, but when you responded in obedience, you discovered there was a process involved and there was much uncertainty involved and you started to feel tricked and trapped by God, felt alone and abandoned because it took so long? If you have not, your time is coming. Situations of sincere obedience to God that bring you into massive uncertainty will reveal you. They will reveal the anger that resides in us. I do not know how many times I have felt anger in my heart towards God when I have felt tricked, abandoned, neglected and left on my own when all I was trying to do is be faithful to His calling and trust Him in obedience. The anger in me has always exposed my old unhealed wounds and my lack of insight into divine purpose and methods. Everything that happens to us today is not new.

What has been will be again, what has been done will be done again; there is nothing new under the sun.

(Ecclesiastes 1:9)

When you look at Jesus' disciples, old testament prophets, Elijah, Elisha, Jonah, Joseph, Moses, they all went through seasons of massive uncertainty in the midst of their obedience to God. Some of them were suicidal, angry and frustrated. David used his frustrations to express his heart to God. He wrote psalms, hymns and songs we can all read and relate to today as a way of expressing his heart. David was honest, but he maintained the fear of God in His heart. If, in our frustration and anger, we start to think God is like one of us and reduce Him to our level, we are being deceived. God is Holy. Everything He does and allows is Holy. We may not understand why, but God has a plan and purpose regardless of how we feel. Faith believes God has a plan even when we feel neglected and abandoned by Him. This takes a lot of intentional effort and it is an effort we must continually make. It will play on our self-importance, but it will help us realize the true importance is seeing yourself in God no matter how you feel. Making this effort to see God truthfully no matter the circumstance is the difference between walking in God's purposes and missing God's purposes in our generation. No matter how many times we fail to get it right and to see God the right way, we ought to continue to make an effort to grow, to repent, to trust God in faith. God is true and cannot lie and that is just the way it is no matter our circumstances. God loves us no matter what. He has good plans for you and everything He allows is helping us walk in His good plans whether we feel it or not.

Nothing shakes hell and the devil like a Christian who believes God, stands on the truth of His character amidst massive confusion and disappointment and anger and frustration. This is called worship! Make your life about standing up for what God stands up for and dismissing what God dismisses. To be in right standing with God is what helps us have an upright look at the things of this world. The truth is the person of Jesus Christ and nothing more. All other passion and anger is misled and misdirected.

Chapter 5

Pursuing the Call

I f you are serious about becoming the person God wants you to be whatever it takes, then you are not holding this book by accident. I am not there yet. In fact, I am far from where I want to be and where I am supposed to finally end up and accomplish for the Kingdom in my lifetime, but I want to continue to share with you my experience thus far. No matter how long you have been involved in ministry, this will either resonate with you as a confirmation or as a light being switched on to illuminate your path as the Holy Spirit brings enlightenment to your journey.

The way the calling of God on our lives unfolds will hardly look like what we imagined. Like I mentioned earlier, you have to start somewhere, anywhere in order to start to discover your calling. When God starts to become specific with you as you seek Him and make Him a priority as you serve, it will evolve into specifics. It will grow into doing what you were created for. God's invitation to follow Him and pursue His specific purpose for us often comes to us when we do not feel adequately prepared or equipped for it, and that is appropriately so. I mean, we are natural people in a natural world following a supernatural God who is spirit. Pursuing your calling from God is treading uncharted, unfamiliar, unnatural territory.

God often talks to me in dreams and visions about what He intends to do and what I should be pursuing. I have learned over the years that God gives us dreams and visions as glimpses of our possible future, and what we could possibly accomplish for the Kingdom, but the actual invitation and unfolding comes to us in raw form. Just because you had a dream about something happening in your life in the future does not mean it is guaranteed to happen. It is going to require the hard work that goes with pursuing your calling. God's call on our lives is not handed to us. It is discovered through years of consistent investment in the things of God and hard work. The way the things of God start and unfold will look so unlike what you imagined, unlike what you saw in dreams and visions that you will start to question God and yourself. You will start to think you did not hear God right, that you made a wrong turn or that you are confused. You will question your own sense of judgment and even your character. The faith walk is an exciting adventure punctuated with much fear, confusion and doubt.

God promised Abraham a son. Abraham waited a while and nothing was happening. At the suggestion of his wife Sarah, they tried to help God make a son for themselves through her maid Hagar. It was not what God promised. God does not need our help to fulfill an impossible promise. What is impossible for us is out of our realm of ability, but is within God's realm of habit. After many years and the mistake with Hagar, God still kept His promise to Abraham. Later, God asked Abraham to sacrifice the very son He gave him.

The reason God allows us to experience the unfolding of His purposes in our lives in the ways that we do is because those circumstances will test our character. They will reveal what is inside of us. They will challenge us to change and to grow. The more we grow, the more we can do for the Kingdom. It gives me hope that Abraham, the father of faith, tried to help God fulfill his purpose, following the advice of his wife, Sarah.

> Now Sarai, Abram's wife had borne him no children. But she had an Egyptian slave named Hagar, so she said to Abram, The Lord has kept me from having children. God sleep with my slave; perhaps I can build a family through her. Abram agreed to what Sarai said.

> **(Genesis 16:1-2)**

I do not know about you, but I have often made assumptions about what I thought God was doing and how He wanted it done, and I have often been sincerely wrong. You can be sincerely wrong in pursuit of God's purpose. This is why we have to be open to the Holy Spirit's guidance. God has given me a slap on the wrist or a knock on the head when I'm going about things wrong, and I have had to stop and ask what and how He really wanted me to do it. This is why we have to be careful with the counsel we receive, make sure you are not taking action at the whim of a moment, and make sure you are not going through motions of ministry, but are continually consulting with God about the right course of action. It is important to pause, think, wait, because God is not in a hurry. He can do what takes us 1000 years in a minute. Our mistakes will help us appreciate our humanity and its limitations and appreciate God's divinity and His unlimitedness. Mistakes are not disqualifications. They are redirections, opportunities to get a new perspective on what works. Our calling often unfolds through mistakes, failures, messes. As we stumble into purpose, there is no straight road to your God-given destiny.

God's instructions will sometimes sound contradicting. He will sometimes ask you to do something in obedience, and then He will ask you to stop doing the very thing He asked you to do. Continuing in it any longer after the new instructions would tantamount to disobedience. God allows contradictions because they test our commitment to staying the course and not getting lost in the motions of ministry. It is so easy to get lost in the motions of ministry, to get into the habit of ministry that it becomes second nature, but is disconnected from the Spirit of God. What God is looking for in order to establish His purpose with us and through us is intimacy.

> Does the Lord delight in burnt offerings and sacrifices as much as in obeying the Lord? To obey is better than sacrifice (ministry), and to heed (paying attention to what God wants in every situation) is better than the fat of rams.

(Is better than going through the motions of ministry)

(1 Samuel 15:22)

The end goal of ministry is not to get the job done. It is to accomplish God's intended purpose for a situation. You could be so sincerely busy in what you call ministry and still miss God's purpose for the moment. Abraham received the promised child, but was later asked to give him up as a sacrifice. Abraham obeyed God to sacrifice Isaac, but as he went about it, if he had carried through with this obedience, not listening to God's continuing instructions, he would have killed Isaac, obeying old instructions that were simply meant as a test of his character. The end goal of obedience in ministry is intimacy. The more we serve God's purposes and pursue His calling on our lives in obedience, the closer we should be getting to Him. If this is not happening, then time to stop and evaluate priorities. Perhaps God has been trying to get your attention, but you are lost in the motions of ministry and cannot hear Him, yet still feel justified with God because you got the job done; you finished that service, preached that sermon. The danger with getting lost in the motions of ministry is we still think we are serving God's purpose, but we are actually lost in the motions of ministry. Do not replace the motions of ministry with the relationship. You risk missing out on the most beautiful relationship you could have this side of life, plus you risk missing your purpose and having all your works burned up.

'Do not lay a hand on the boy,' he said. 'Do not do anything to him. Now I know that you fear God,

95

because you have not withheld from me your son, your only son.' Abraham looked up and there in a thicket he saw a ram caught by its horns. He went over and took the ram and sacrificed it as a burnt offering instead of his son. So Abraham called that place The Lord Will Provide. And to this day, it is said, 'On the mountain of the Lord, it will be provided.'

(Genesis 22:12-14)

Did I miss God?

I don't know how many times I have asked myself this question. I know it has been countless times. I said earlier that I planted Musaale Church in Eastern Uganda with a bunch of friends on January 26th, 2014.

Before we planted the church, I asked God to give me a date to start, but He did not. I asked God to show me His chosen, 'anointed' venue we could use to launch the church and still got no response. I then thought, if God won't tell me, I am going to decide the date and look for a possible venue and start services. I will only stop if God says to stop. So I did that, and after we launched the church, God said you're on track, son.

It dawned on me then just how much I had 'spiritualized' everything and just how religious I was in my devotion to God. You can be devoted to God, but still miss it if you place God in a box of how He works. God doesn't give a lot of details. We must be creative and practical. Just go and I will show you when you get there. The walk of faith is punctuated with much uncertainty and requires much creativity.

There are things God will tell you directly how and when to do, but following God, most of the time, I have learned He will give you general directions on what to do and it will be up to us to figure out how to make it happen. Here's what happens as we go about figuring things out; Our hearts are exposed, cracks are revealed, motives are revealed, our own lack of insight on life and things are revealed, weaknesses are revealed. You can be so exposed to the point you start to lose hope in yourself because you feel completely incapable and unqualified for the task God has called you to fulfill. Here is the good thing about this revelation; When we recognize our shortcomings, we start to recognize our true source of strength. This is when we start to place all our confidence in God. You will start to rely on God like never before when He calls you into situations that reveal your limitations. The exposure is not a dismissal or a reprimand, though it may feel that way sometimes. It is simply a revelation of truth, a redirection. An opportunity to open up and surrender to the one who does the impossible more and more. The things of God can only be built in consultation with God because in our own fickle, flesh and bones strength, we are incapable of making any lasting, eternal and divine impact. The Spirit gives life, but the flesh counts for nothing - Jesus.

The devil works full time to discourage us when our shortcomings are exposed. He will whisper in our ear, "You do not have what it takes for this. You cannot do this. If you could do it, you could already have done this or that as others already have. Plus, you would not have these weaknesses.

People who accomplish the things you are going after do not have these weaknesses." The devil is a liar! The truth is, what we are not, God is for us and more. I have sometimes bought into the lies of the devil and been so hard on myself for the weaknesses I have seen within, but then I have also realized being hard on me never helps. It only does the devil's job of false accuser for him. God is our strength, our hope, our victory is in Him and from Him, our success comes from Him, we are more than conquerors as long as we are in the one who conquered death and loves us so dearly. Hallelujah, somebody!

> We do not want you to be uninformed, brothers and sisters, about the troubles we experienced in the province of Asia. We were under great pressure, far beyond our ability to endure, so that we despaired of life itself. Indeed, we felt we had received the sentence of death. But this happened that we might not rely on ourselves but on God, who raises the dead. He has delivered us from such a deadly peril, and he will deliver us again. On him, we have set our hope that he will continue to deliver us, as you help us by your prayers. Then many will give thanks on our behalf for the gracious favor granted us in answer to the prayers of many.

(2 Corinthians 1:8-11)

God doesn't give us details about our purpose because He knows we might not take the journey if we know what lies ahead. We would be too afraid to walk by faith if we knew some of the uncertainties and troubles and sufferings that awaited us. We would also miss the amazing beauty that comes out of walking by faith. Many people who avoid the road less traveled, who choose safety instead, miss out on the most amazing life experience one could ever have on planet earth. They also stay spiritually stunted.

Following the call of God on your life is not convenient or comfortable. In fact, the uncertainty of the journey can be frighteningly scary. The rejection you experience as you go can be painful. Jesus was sent to save humanity from our sins, but was rejected from the first day He declared His purpose in Luke 4:18. One of the things that will test our faith as we pursue God's calling on our lives the most is having to explain our calling to those we already know and think will support us but find they do not believe we are called to that specific purpose. When God called me to return to my hometown and plant a life-giving church, I knew that it was something I had always wanted to do. When I spoke to some people who knew me about it, they said it was a mistake, said my life was already headed in the right direction and working out well and this was a distraction bound to fail. They were somewhat right. My safari business was growing by leaps and bounds. When it comes to the purpose of God for our lives, we do not ask people's opinions on what to do. We inform them of what we are doing because we have already heard from God. You do not need anyone's permission to pursue the call of God on your life.

When we launched Musaale church in the most happening town, a.k.a Mbale, we were treated with suspicion by existing churches. They called us a cult and made all kinds of false accusations to discredit our ministry, but I knew who had called me. Whether people liked our church or me did not matter. Whatever they said did not matter as long as I was in the center of God's will, doing what God called me to do. God had brought me a long way to get me to the place where I did not care what people thought about me. Before God deploys you, He will do a work in you that prepares you for what He is calling you to. The church has since outgrown a number of the churches that said all kinds of things about us, plus some have had a change of heart after interacting with us and witnessing who we really are and what we are all about. Most of the people who dismiss your calling do not know you. This is why you only need the audience and opinion of the ONE who created you and knows you fully, plus those he places in your life who are confidants and believe in you, if you are going to walk in your calling.

When God asked me to leave the two church campuses I planted in Uganda and come to the United States at the end of 2019, I wrestled with the idea. I wrestled with planting our second campus in Soroti, but not like coming to America by faith. Like I mentioned earlier, I have been to most of the United States for over 17 years, but usually on a scheduled itinerary. This time God was asking me to come out by faith with no scheduled itinerary. Besides, 2019 was a tough year for me financially as we did not have much in safari bookings at my business. I did not have money. I said to God, I won't be able to go this time as I cannot afford the air ticket. Well, that was no sufficient excuse because the air ticket money showed up. I then said to God, I need money for my accommodation, transport, meals etc. God was silent about that. He simply said, go! I delayed, thinking I wasn't hearing right, but I got the same message, go!

Touring the world with the Watoto choir was scheduled for many months at a time with accommodations organized through the churches we performed at. Since I left the choir, my trips to America have always been self-funded, staying at Airbnb bookings and using car rentals for getting around. I have only had accommodation arranged when I have visited at an invitation to Virginia Beach, Virginia or Houston, Texas or Green Bay, Wisconsin to preach at a church and or school. This time God was asking me to make the trip to America with no schedule arranged. I wrestled with it until God won. I came out thinking since God called me, He will make a way and everything will be laid out for me.

Well, it was not and has not been clearly laid out for me. I have taken a day at a time, trusting, hoping, doubting, not knowing, fearing, believing, learning, meeting people, exploring. I have had to get back to the drawing board of my life and ask myself if I really know who God is. When God calls you and places you in circumstances beyond your control that you do not understand, and it looks like He who called you is doing nothing about your situation, it will rattle you. When you reach out to ask for support and the ones you expect to help suspect your true intentions, it will rattle you. It will also reveal you and grow you and give you a new perspective on life and people and how they fit in your life. Trusting God in faith in the middle of uncertainty will make you very vulnerable and susceptible to the lies of the enemy. In my situation, I have found that even though I have complete confidence in God's ability to do anything, I have thought myself to be the missing ingredient. I have thought, perhaps God is not doing certain things for me because I do not have the character for it. I cannot be trusted with it. I have thought myself unqualified and incapable of pursuing the call of God on my life because I lack the required personality skills for it. The devil likes this kind of thinking in us a lot. He knows he doesn't have to do much to stop us because we are already discrediting ourselves and disqualifying ourselves from a calling a perfect God in His grace and mercy has already qualified us for.

You will always think you are just fine and well equipped for the call of God on your life until you are placed in the fire. When in the fire, we not only discover our weaknesses, we discover God's strength. In fact, even though I do not enjoy the difficult circumstances God has allowed me to face, they have benefited me more than they have hurt me. They have opened my eyes and my mind to what truly matters, to how to deal with people, to where people are, to who God is and to who I am. You see, when you are in the midst of struggle, you tend to think you are the only one going through it. But you will discover as you go that the ones you thought neglected you also need your help. They need your prayers. They need your encouragement. This is how your true ministry impact for the Kingdom is born. You find purpose in the midst of your struggles. The people who seem to neglect you, did not neglect you. They just could not help you. Those who neglect you when they could help you are not meant to help you or they are just people with bad ideas that hinder their generosity and ability to connect. God said to me, *"There's no bad people, just people with bad ideas."*

If you make your struggles and difficult circumstances about you and victimize yourself as you pursue God's calling, you will miss your purpose in the midst of the circumstances you face. This is what the devil would love for us to do. Nothing irks the devil like one who continues to be peaceful and persistent in their calling in the face of rejection and struggle. Jesus went through all of this and more, He was called demon-possessed and raving mad by those HE came to save and He said if people did that to Him, they would do the same to us who follow Him. I wish God did things another way, making it smoother to pursue His call on our lives, but no. His way is perfect. We learn to truly worship God and genuinely and satisfactorily fulfill our purpose through the difficulties we face. All else is child's play.

> *I will proclaim the name of the Lord. Oh, praise the greatness of our God! He is a rock, His works are perfect and all His ways are just. A faithful God who does no wrong, upright and just is He.*

(Deuteronomy 32:3-4)

Called to an adventure!

God's call always invites us into an adventure. Not knowing how God is going to do the things He said He is going to do is the adventure. If you like to be in control of how things are going to happen, and most of us like to be, following Jesus will shake that real good. God invites us to loosen up and live. I tend to be a spontaneous person, but God has shaken even that to the bone. God said to me once, *"If you knew everything I was going to do upfront, it would not be an adventure, then would it?"* I said it would not, but it would be nice to have some more details, Sir! I have said to God many times in our conversations; Why don't You talk to me like You did Joseph? Do not divorce Mary. She is pregnant by the power of the Holy Spirit. She is not lying to you. You will keep her as your wife, but do not sleep with her until she has had the world-saving baby. You will call Him Jesus when He is born and He will save humanity from their sins. Or in another instance, "Joseph, Get up, flee to Egypt, stay there a while. Herod is looking to kill the child." and Joseph did. That's real clear communication and instruction, right?

But, I'm sure Joseph was still confused as we humans get when we don't know or see the full picture of what we are called to do. We do not read it in the scriptures, but he must have wondered why he had to flee to Egypt when he had God with him. The God who owns the world and has legions of Angels with ready fire swords. Surely God would protect Himself, right? Perplexing stuff, ha! God doesn't break His own rules or change His principles, not even for Himself. If God did, Joseph and Mary would have failed to fulfill their purpose. Plus, God would not need us. There would be no reward for faithfulness. Not even Jesus was getting an easy pass. If God changed the rules for you and for me, making things easier and convenient, our lives would be boring and purposeless.

When you read the story of Mary and Joseph, you don't see this. It is only when you start following God's instructions in your own life that you start to place yourself in the shoes of Mary and Joseph. It was not an easy or convenient purpose having and raising Jesus, but what an eternally fulfilling responsibility they had. We are talking about them and the world-saving baby millenniums later.

We do not get to hear about how Joseph and Mary spent their lives in Egypt, but the gifts they received of gold, frankincense and myrrh at Christ's birth were worth millions of dollars. They went to Egypt as wealthy people. They were fleeing Herod, but it was also an adventure for them because they had spending power. They probably purchased a boat and took baby Jesus on a cruise down the Nile River every once in a while. Don't you think? Never mind! That's just my wild imagination, but you get the point. There was an inconvenience, discomfort for Mary and Joseph accompanied with blessings to them and to the world at the birth of Jesus. Many people want the blessings of God, but are not faithful when faced with the struggles and inconveniences that come with the stewardship of the calling.

> On coming to the house, they saw the child with his mother Mary, and they bowed down and worshipped him. Then they opened their treasures and presented him with gifts of gold, frankincense and myrrh.

> **(Matthew 2:11)**

Even though there is suffering to endure when following Jesus and pursuing your calling, I take issue with people who think that following Jesus is all suffering, so they avoid all the fun stuff because it distracts from the mission. Suffering is part of life and every one of us will experience our fair share of it, but ministry is not all suffering for Jesus. Manufactured, self-imposed suffering is not from God. Everything God allows is balanced in proportion to the purpose we are meant to fulfill. Mary and Joseph faced ridicule because of Mary getting pregnant out of wedlock. Joseph considered ending the relationship quietly, but an angel appeared to him and said, carry on with it, name the child Jesus. We don't get to see it when we read the Bible, the actual responses from people, the attitudes they carried towards Mary and Joseph. I'm sure Mary lost friends for having the Savior of the world, Joseph lost friends for choosing to believe what Mary said over his friends and for following the angel's instructions. Mary risked losing her life by stoning for having Jesus. We get to read this part of the Bible. Joseph must have been labeled a loser by his contemporaries for choosing to marry a woman who was already pregnant and the pregnancy wasn't his. The life God offers won't be convenient or easy, but it will be purposeful and meaningful. Plus, there will be loads and loads of adventure along with the pain and suffering that comes with it.

I said in the introduction that my family was poor as a church mouse. Well, for being from such a poor family, I have had life experiences that only a small percentage of the human population can afford. I have been to most parts of the world. I have been to 44 states across America, not counting two that I just went through recently. I cannot begin to count the cities. Don't ask my favorite state, but I'm in love with Hawaii. I have been everywhere in Australia, most parts of Canada, including in minus 45 degrees Celsius temperatures in a town called Shawinigan in Quebec. I have been to just about every part of the United Kingdom, most of New Zealand, Japan and Taiwan. I have also been to Beijing, China, Hong Kong, South Africa, Swaziland, Tanzania, Kenya, Rwanda, Zambia,

Zimbabwe, United Arab Emirates, plus dropped into Singapore, Malaysia, Italy, Mozambique. It's been a wild ride and I wouldn't trade it for anything in the whole wide world. I'm just glad I said yes to Jesus. Glad that I embraced God's call on my life, and even with the discomfort, the uncertainty and inconvenience and the suffering involved, I will keep taking God on His offers till I fly into eternity to spend forever with Jesus.

I have hosted many mission teams to Uganda through my safari business and I'm often disappointed when people say they don't want to go on safari and stay in a nice lodge because it takes away from their mission. I personally find that religious. Not because I miss out on making money, but because God created this world and its creatures for us to enjoy, marvel at and be refreshed. The more refreshed we are, the more effective we can be on the mission God has called us on. Thou shalt not manufacture suffering for Jesus.

Most people in ministry burn out because they are trying to outdo Jesus working so hard. We ought to remember Jesus' first miracle was at a party turning water into wine. The Pharisees regularly accused Christ and His disciples of having too much fun, eating and drinking with tax collectors and sinners and gluttons.

As we follow the path God calls us on, we will find He cares for the fine details of our lives and will sometimes direct us to do nothing. Sometimes God tells me to wake up and visit a waterfall and do absolutely nothing but relax for the day. There is someone reading this who is in ministry and is asking, does God really say that to you? Yes indeed! I have discovered why God does that. God knows when we need to relax and when we need to work hard. God has an aerial and inside view of our lives and how we are progressing and are meant to progress. He knows us better than we know ourselves. God knows how we were created to function. He created us!

If we only care to pay attention to God's leading at all times, He wants to guide us in all things. We often think that God will only guide us in important decisions, but God cares about everything that concerns us to the last-minute detail. Our calling is fulfilled in concert with our relationship of intimacy with Jesus. Without the intimacy, you are bound to get lost in the motions of ministry.

Chapter 6

The Big Picture

When we planted our first church campus in the most happening town, I was excited to bring a new church culture into my hometown. I expected that many people would be excited along with me and come running to the party. It wasn't the case. I quickly learned something about what God was doing. While I was focused on planting and establishing a life-giving church with great music and great preaching, God was focusing on planting me and giving me the life I had always dreamed of. He was focused on challenging me to become all I was meant to be in Him and challenging those who would come, who had embraced a shallow faith in Him. God wanted me to create a place where He would corner people and get them to face things they had been running away from for years. You see, God had cornered me like I shared earlier and brought me to a place of broken surrender. It was time for me to create a place for Him to do the same in other people's lives. Jesus never said to go out into all the world and plant churches. He said to go out into all the world and make disciples. Go and multiply your experiences with ME. Planting a church is easier than making disciples. The goal of planting churches should be to make more disciples of Christ. Making disciples means getting into the greasy, messy parts of people's lives. It means confronting people when God says to. It means losing face with people regularly because of your actions on behalf of God.

God said to me when the church started to grow and people started to call it a church family; You are not a family yet, son! I said to God; But isn't that what your church is? He said to me; Family is people who annoy each other, get on each other's nerves, offend each other, almost want to kill each other, but they forgive each other and grow together. That is family, son.

I looked at the team I had at the time and we had not shared any annoying moments, heartbreaking moments. We had not offended each other deeply and reached the point of wanting to kill each other. Some walked on eggshells to keep the peace and avoid offense, we were surface-level shallow and God hates shallow.

Slowly God started to ask me to challenge people. You see, Christ said, "Blessed are the peacemakers," not peacekeepers.

Peacekeeping involves avoiding conflict by all means. Peacemaking, on the other hand, involves rocking the boat, challenging the status quo, creating conflict in order to confront and get rid of the superficial in the church. God doesn't work among the superficial. That is territory for the devil, who is a masquerader, a pretender, and a fake. He loves superficial environments because that is where deception thrives. The devil is a liar!

God usually gives everyone a chance to deal with our sins and issues privately with Him. But when we insist on our ways and don't make an effort to change even with His persistent warnings, He exposes us for our own good. So God started to expose the private lives of people on my team, plus asked me to get them to step down from being part of the team, but they could stay and attend church services if they wanted to. The church is not a social club. It is the blood-bought family of the creator of Heaven and earth. It cost Christ His life and you cannot claim to serve Him and still live your life any way you want. God wanted a higher commitment to character from everyone on the team. Our life in Christ is not our own. We have been bought at the highest price.

You can be popular with people as a pastor when you do not rock the boat, when you simply accept everyone without challenging them. You can be a star like that. Unfortunately, you will be your own star building your own kingdom and not the Kingdom of Heaven on earth. God confronts us to confront others on His behalf.

I quickly started to become unpopular as a pastor when I started asking people to step down and focus more on their personal walk with God. Talented people, committed people. They were more committed to the church and to ministry than they were to God. The church gave them an opportunity to engage their talent, but they were not taking their relationship with God seriously. There was compromise in their lives. They had sex outside marriage, deliberately cheated and lied, among other things. You see, God will accommodate weakness in our lives, but not intentional sin. Like I shared in Paul's appeal to the Ephesian church earlier, there are things we must let go of and not just pray about if we are going to be the people God wants us to be. Weakness will always be in our lives as a result of our human condition. God makes room for that, but not for deliberate compromise we refuse to give up.

Talking about weakness, when God started asking me to challenge people, I must say it was not comfortable. It made me do some personal soul searching. I found myself giving excuses to God of I'm a sinner too. This may be true and may even sound humble, but God said to me, "So you are having sex outside marriage and cheating people of their money too? I said no sir! You know I am not. He said then deal with these individuals. This is when I started to confront another one of my own issues, which was people-pleasing. I wasn't willing to confront people not because I approved or condoned their deliberate sin or that I practiced it myself, but because I was a people pleaser. Saul lost his mandate with God as king over Israel because he was a people pleaser. We lose our credibility with God in ministry when we want to please everyone. Someone once said, "If you want to please everyone, do not be a pastor. Go and sell Ice cream."

Then Saul said to Samuel, 'I have sinned. I violated the Lord's command and your instructions. I was afraid of the men and so I gave in to them. Now I beg you, forgive my sin and come back with me, so that I may worship the Lord.' But Samuel said to him, 'I will not go back with you. You have rejected the word of the Lord, and the Lord has rejected you as king over Israel!' As Samuel turned to leave, Saul caught hold of the hem of his robe, and it tore. Samuel said to him, 'The Lord has torn the kingdom of Israel from you today and has given it to one of your neighbors – to one better than you. He who is the Glory of Israel does not lie or change his mind; for he is not a human being, that he should change his mind.'

(1 Samuel 15:24-29)

I think life's biggest miss is to miss God's purpose for you. The second biggest miss, I think, is to find your calling, but pursue doing God's will in a way He doesn't approve of. I felt like a Saul at that moment; I was afraid to challenge people. So I said to myself, even though I kind of feel like Saul at this moment, I want to be like David. I know I am a David! I said I would do it afraid, so the confrontation started. After all, even though I planted it, this was still not my church. I thought it was God's church. This was not my idea to plant a church. It was His. Then I feared I was going to lose members just when I was starting to build up some numbers in regular attendance, but doing God's will God's way was more important to me than having a lot of pew warmers. I said I would take action. God would be responsible for the consequences. Walk in obedience and let God be responsible for the unpopular actions you take to honor Him.

To my surprise, just when I thought confrontation would cut on church attendance numbers, when I started to confront people for their deliberately sinful lifestyles, asking them to step down from being involved on the team, even with their threats that the church would collapse without them, the numbers in the church started to grow even more. I always knew that the church was not my thing, but God's thing, but I had not really understood how much this was true. God's church is built God's way, not by our programs, not our way at all. God brings some and He removes some. He has a rhythm and we must get with God's rhythm. God builds numbers by subtraction.

> Now I say to you that you are Peter (which means 'rock'), and upon this rock I will build my church, and all the powers of hell will not conquer it. And I will give you the keys of the Kingdom of Heaven. Whatever you forbid[h] on earth will be forbidden in heaven, and whatever you permit on earth will be permitted in heaven."

(Matthew 16:18-19)

God builds His church on revelation, on the basis of personal experience. He builds it with those who know Him and will represent Him unapologetically. Saul wanted to be in the people's good favor as well as God's good favor. I have found out on my own journey that you cannot pull this off however heroic you try to be. Not even Batman or Ironman or Superman in make-believe movies where anything is possible can pull this move off. Now I have been called Batman before because I'm bad, okay, not that bad, but I wasn't going to try to be Batman for the church of Jesus Christ. There has to come a point in each of our lives when we decide who we are going to unapologetically live for, Peoples approval or the approval of Jesus. For me, this was a no brainer. I chose Jesus. I made my decision that I would live to please God, no matter what that meant, even if I were alone. I would make uncomfortable, costly and inconvenient decisions as long as He said to make them. I was willing to lose people's favor for the sake of doing God's will. I was willing to have people say all kinds of things about me, calling me all sorts of names, but I was not going to be a Saul.

I said to my team, "I don't mind doing the music alone, preaching, moderating the service if that's what it comes down to. I need commitment to God, not to the church. I started to discover that when you start to confront the people God asks you to confront, the superficial starts to lose ground. Genuine people who are intent on living for God started to emerge and start coming in and wanting to commit to the house. Plus, those who were are on the team, but sitting on the edge testing the waters with one foot, got off the edge and jumped in with both feet and started to take their commitment to God seriously.

> *"No one can serve two masters. Either you will hate the one and love the other, or you will be devoted to the one and despise the other. You cannot serve both God and money.*

> **(Matthew 6:24)**

Everything God does outside of us, He does inside of us first. There is no overnight success with God. There is seed time and pruning and nurturing and more pruning and endurance and then harvest and we must learn to trust God's

115

rhythm, plus submit and run with it if we are going to see the fulfillment of His promise to work wonders among us. God said to me, *"You will only take people spiritually to a place you have been to spiritually yourself. You cannot give what you do not have."*

A very sobering statement indeed! God says it as it is, no filter, no mincing words. The experiences God calls us on and we follow obediently, He wants to use to place something in us that we can then turn around and give to the people we lead. The pain you go through as a leader is not a waste of time. It is an investment. God will never call you to something He has not gifted and equipped you for.

The more we go through with God, the more He can deposit in us and entrust us with. The process comes before the trust. I wish I could say it is easy to go through the painful seasons. It never is, at least not for me. You will want to give up. You will wish to be taken to Heaven. I don't know how many times I have wished for that. I have also realized I always think that way on the days when I completely don't seem to understand what God is doing. When I want to be the best I can be, honoring God, but I still don't seem to get it, those are the moments I often wish for a transfer to Heaven. God will only trust us to the extent He can prune us and we can endure the pain of transformation.

Everything God does is focused on the big picture of our lives. While I was focused on how many would come to church, God was and is focused on how many would really get what God was on about and that I myself really got what I was on about.

Our church slogan is, *"Changing the world with the love of Jesus."*

Our mission is *"To equip the church for the work of the Kingdom so that together we can establish the Father's will on earth as it is in Heaven."*

When God called Moses to lead the tribe of Israel out of Egypt to the promised land, He knew Moses had spent 40 years in the palace as Prince of Egypt and 40 years in the wilderness looking after sheep. It was familiar territory for him both ways. Have you ever thought about this? Moses was the first official megachurch pastor. His mission was to rescue Israel to go and worship the Lord their God away from Egypt. They were leaving Egypt to plant a church.

Moses had a congregation of over 3 million people as soon as Israel left Egypt and crossed the Red Sea. Moses, who was raised as a prince in Egypt, became a leader for Israel. It was all as God intended it for him. If you look carefully at the lives of old testament Bible prophets and leaders, they all bear the DNA of church leaders. God has always been about having a family on earth. Israel was God's first Church on planet earth, but today His church is composed of people of all races, colors, nations, backgrounds. The big picture of every single church family nucleus on earth is to create a little Heaven on earth, God's family where His spirit works and rules and orders the lives of people establishing His will and His Kingdom one person at a time.

Chapter 7

Take It or Leave It!

God knows what we were created to do and to be in this world, so He does not need to consult or negotiate with us on the best course of action when it comes to fulfilling our divine purpose. God is not up in Heaven negotiating with us on the best possible way to do things. He is up in Heaven saying, "This is how it's done." God's calling is a take it or leave it kind of thing. Even though God does not consult us on the best course of action, God does not force His will on anyone. You have to voluntarily want it, desire it, and willingly go after it. God will not plead with us over our calling. He can find someone else to use if we do not obey. There is no partly in and partly out with God. Our God is an "extremist." You are either completely in or completely out, not half in half out. One foot in to test the waters, see if it works out, while one foot out at the ready to jump out when it gets uncomfortable. When you give yourself fully to pursuing God's call on your life, it will open you up to a supernatural world with God, one people who stay on the sidelines miss. The unfolding of my own journey pursuing God's purpose for my life has caused me to look deeper into Moses' life, plus to empathize with him and other characters God used in the Bible. The Bible was not given to us just for reference, but for demonstration purposes. We can understand our own journey by looking at the journeys of Bible characters. When God calls us to pursue our purpose, it sort of looks like when He called Moses.

> *The Lord said, "I have indeed seen the misery of my people in Egypt. I have heard them crying out because of their slave drivers, and I am concerned about their suffering. So I have come down to rescue them from the hand of the Egyptians and to bring them up out of that land into a good and spacious land, a land flowing with milk and honey—the home of the Canaanites, Hittites, Amorites, Perizzites, Hivites and Jebusites. And now the cry of the Israelites has reached me, and I have seen the way the Egyptians are oppressing them. So now, go. I am sending you to Pharaoh to bring my people the Israelites out of Egypt."*

(Exodus 3:7-10)

God appeared to Moses in a bush fire that wasn't going out. Moses drew near to this strange never before seen sight and then the exchange started.

When God started talking about rescuing His people Israel, this is what I think was going on in Moses' mind; Wow, God, I tried to help those poor guys 40 years ago, I even killed an

Egyptian man. My effort was pitiful and I did not accomplish much. I ended up running for my life. I met up with Jethro here in Median when I fled Egypt, married his daughter Zipporah and I have been happy looking after sheep. I even own a few of my own. Life did not turn out too bad after all, for this once Prince of Egypt turned fugitive. Now that you want to rescue them, I know you will succeed God. I've never seen a God who sets a bush on fire and it still doesn't burn up. Go for it, Sir, more power God! But as the conversation continues, God says, I am sending you Moses! You tried it on your own last time, and now you get to do it with ME. Whaaaaaat! Not me, said Moses. I'm not qualified to do this.

But Moses said to God, "Who am I that I should go to Pharaoh and bring the Israelites out of Egypt?"

(Exodus 3:11)

Moses had become the perfect candidate for God to work with after 40 years in the wilderness. God will often use our own wilderness seasons to empty us of ourselves. To bring us to a place where we recognize our inadequacy so that we can depend fully on God's power. The desert place will win us of depending on and putting confidence in temporary, material and fleeting things of this world or placing our trust in the wrong places or people or in our own strength.

Earlier, when Moses tried to take matters into his own hands and killed an Egyptian, God knew about it. Brother Moses was acting in the flesh. God will allow us to take matters into our own hands, fail and come to the end of ourselves. Then, He will begin to show us how it works.

When Moses fled Egypt and ended up in Median, it was God who ordered his steps. Moses may not have known it, but God did. When he married Jethro's daughter, God knew it, set Moses up, God expected it and Moses did not disappoint, even had some sons to show for it. But Moses did not know that God had ordered all of this. In fact, when Moses gave the excuse of not being able to talk, God knew the real excuse was that Moses was afraid he would be arrested and incarcerated on arrival in Egypt. He had fled Egypt 40 years earlier after killing a man. We can fool people with our excuses, but not God.

When God calls us on a mission, He wants us to own that mission. We have a stake in the things of God. One day, God will reward us for what we do on this earth on behalf of the Kingdom, but first, we must own it. God will not do His work among men without involving men. That's why Jesus was another type of Moses. I am sure the conversation with Jesus in Heaven was kind of similar to the one with Moses.

"Hey, Jesus!" "Yeah, Dad!" "I have seen the depravity and fallenness of mankind. Their constant and futile attempts to be right with Me, and it's not working for them. This Lucifer guy has them under his shackles. Besides, if they continue with all these sacrifices for their sins, they will soon have no beef to eat. Cows, sheep, goats will become extinct. They will have no barbecues and I care for these people. I love it when they enjoy what I blessed them with in My creation.

Hey son, I want to rescue them once and for all and I AM sending you. Will you go for us, son?"

It was different with Jesus. He immediately said, "Sure, DAD." Then God added, "You will become like one of them, you will dwell in a womb of a young lady I will choose and like one of the humans after nine months be born just like they do. You will then grow up with this young lady and a young man I will choose. They will be your parents. That way, you will get to experience everything the humans experience and you will feel their struggles, their hopelessness, their depravity, so when you become their ransom, you will know exactly what it is you will be dying for. Will you still do it, son?" "Yes, DAD, It's a tough ask to leave streets of gold and descend into dusty paths among filthy, sick humans, but I'll still do it for us Dad, when do we start?" "Soon son, very soon!" Fast forward, and that's how we got Christmas!

The circumstances under which Jesus was born were not comfortable. He was born in a manger, in a Kraal. That's how the Savior of the world made His grand entrance on planet earth. This goes to show that it doesn't matter where you are born, who your earthly father or your family is; you can change the world if you choose to follow Jesus and wholeheartedly do the will of God the Father.

What limits us the most in the church is the things we hold on to. Moses had to confront and let go of his past as a prince of Egypt who became a fugitive, so that he would go on and become the deliverer of the nation of Israel. God knew this. When Moses got to Egypt, he probably thought, they might remember I killed someone and arrest me, but it did not happen. He then probably thought, 'I will be on my way, get to Egypt, talk to Pharaoh under God's awesome power and all Israel with me, rescued." "I will turn my rod into a snake and Pharaoh won't know what hit him. He will run for his life. I will pick up the snake by the tail, and it will turn back into a rod and Pharaoh, petrified by my rod become snake, will pronounce an immediate release for the children of Israel. After all, who has ever turned a rod into a snake before?"

But the story was much different than that. Pharaoh's witch doctors also made their own snakes and Moses thought, "Whaaat?? God, you gave them my trick! Why?" His snake ate their snakes in a demonstration of superiority, but Pharaoh was not impressed. Days turned into weeks and weeks turned to months. Pharaoh's heart was hard and God who sent Moses had something to do with it. Can you relate to Moses? I can! When God asked me to leave the church I planted in Uganda and come to America, I had this thought in mind that everything would be laid out for me and what He was calling me to do would be prearranged for me to fit into it like a glove. I had some dreams before embarking on the mission, which seemed to imply I would hit the ground running, but far from it! God gives us dreams and visions to reveal the future. The dreams just don't tell us there is an immediate process involved and there are bridges to cross.

Moses had to embrace his calling and the complicated details involved. He could not turn back. He was in it and had to keep going, just like I accepted my calling along with the discomfort involved. Do not stop being faithful in pursuing God's call and assignment on your life because it has gotten difficult and you do not understand what is going on anymore. God knows what is going on and that should be enough for us. This is easier said than done. It takes effort to keep going when things do not make sense. Pursuing your calling with God is always fun and games until you come to the place where nothing makes sense, where it feels like the God who called you is has abandoned you and is holding out on you.

No God like Jehovah!

Moses knew Pharaoh would not listen to him. God had warned him. In fact, God said He would harden Pharaoh's heart. I tried to understand the meaning of this and struggled with it for years in my journey pursuing divine purpose. I couldn't understand why God would give you an assignment and then make it really hard to accomplish. I have since come to the conclusion; Pharaoh was already an arrogant man. He was leading the most powerful nation on earth at the time. His confidence was in the strength of his nation built on the free labor of the sweat of God's chosen people Israel.

Besides, Pharaoh worshiped his own Egyptian idol gods. God had to make a statement. More like prove a point that there is no God like Jehovah! God takes time to make things happen because the detailed lessons involved in the waiting are necessary for all involved. God had a lesson for Pharaoh. He also had lessons Moses needed to learn that would be needed for the journey ahead. Moses was learning faith and patience. Faith doesn't make things easy. It makes them possible. The journey in the wilderness leading the children of Israel would demand the lessons of faith and patience. If God did things our way, we would think we are the best thing that ever happened to planet earth. Moses would have turned out like Pharaoh after it was all said and done. God paces us so that His glory will be revealed in us and through us and we will not glory in the flesh. While God is helping us win in life, He is also winning us of ourselves.

> *The Lord had said to Moses, "Pharaoh will refuse to listen to you—so that my wonders may be multiplied in Egypt." Moses and Aaron performed all these wonders before Pharaoh, but the Lord hardened Pharaoh's heart, and he would not let the Israelites go out of his country.*

(Exodus 11:9-10)

Did you know that God wants to prove a point? He wants to do something in the lives of those he calls His own so the world will hear of it and revere His name. God is not democratic, wanting to please all, but He is not despotic either. God is HOLY! He has no agenda but what is best for humanity.

It was about time for the proud nation of Egypt to be put in its rightful place, for the idol gods to be proven for what they were; Even though they could manufacture their own snakes to match Moses, they were fake and unable to save anyone. It was time for Israel to walk free. The 400 years where God mentioned to Abraham in Genesis 15 about the children of Israel being slaves in a foreign land were over, and it was time for the church to be born on planet earth and for the whole world to hear of it. It was about time for Egypt to realize that all power and all blessings are accumulated because of the benevolent creator of Heaven and earth who has provided a conducive environment for men to be able to work and prosper in their work. He lets the sun shine and the rain fall on the pastor's roof as well as the witch doctor's roof. That's grace! It was time for Pharaoh and Egypt to know that science does not discredit God, but finds its purpose from God. He is the source of all science. He created all the raw materials that give science a purpose.

When Moses, under God's power, led Israel on dry ground across the Red Sea and yet Pharaoh and his army in attempting to pursue drowned, it was a statement to the world, a defying of the laws of science and nature. God was saying, I am boss of all things! The calling of God on your life is meant to tell a story to the world about the greatness and awesomeness of our God.

All the surrounding nations heard about Israel crossing the Red Sea on dry ground and trembled. They had never heard of a God who could pull this off. God wants to astound the world and win people to Himself through the things He does with you and through you as you go about pursuing His call on your life. The only reason God calls us is not just for us to have a purpose, but for His glory to be revealed. Everywhere Israel went, without Facebook or Instagram selfie posts from the children of Israel documenting the miraculous crossing of the Red Sea on dry ground, the news had spread to the nations and they were frightened to face any army that was led by this God - Jehovah! There was no God among their idol gods like Jehovah.

> "I know that the Lord has given you this land and that a great fear of you has fallen on us, so that all who live in this country are melting in fear because of you. We have heard how the Lord dried up the

water of the Red Sea[a] for you when you came out of Egypt, and what you did to Sihon and Og, the two kings of the Amorites east of the Jordan, whom you completely destroyed. When we heard of it, our hearts melted in fear and everyone's courage failed because of you, for the Lord your God is God in heaven above and on the earth below.

(Joshua 2:8-11)

God does not waste anything He does. Everything has purpose to it; that the nations will know His name. We are most blessed and privileged when God calls us to be involved in what He is doing on planet earth.

Moses embraced his calling reluctantly, but saw it through along with the delays and frustrations and challenges he faced because of Pharaoh's hardened heart. Many plagues later, Israel was free to leave. Even after they were pronounced free to leave, they were not really free to leave. Pharaoh pursued from behind. Reminds me of the animation Kungfu Panda where Master Shifu has Po on rapid training to learn the secrets of Kungfu because he was destined to face a strong adversary - Tai lung who had escaped a maximum prison. At the end of the day's training, Shifu says to Po, "You are free to eat." But as Po reaches for a dumpling, Shifu snatches it from him and they play dumpling shuffle. Shifu again says to Po, "You are free to eat!" To which Po responds this time; "I'm I???" Don't want to get distracted, let's carry on.

As Israel sang songs of deliverance on their way out of Egypt, they looked back and saw dust rising to the skies and the Egyptian army pursuing them to return them to the life of slavery. Moses was scared, all of Israel was petrified, but even then, God was not finished with delivering His lessons to Pharaoh. Moses and Israel were about to witness something impossible, a boost of faith. The calling of God will frighten you, it will reveal you, it will build you, and you will witness miracles in the center of divine purpose. I once heard Lisa Bevere preach saying; God let Pharaoh and his army drown in the Red Sea because centuries before that, Egypt had killed Israel's army in taking the lives of male children. I believe that's true. God is thorough in His lessons. He leaves no stone unturned.

Moses' life is an example for us, but Christ Jesus and His birth, His life and His death on the cross and resurrection from the dead would become God's ultimate example to us of what embracing our call in God will look like.

> For those God foreknew he also predestined to be conformed to the image of his Son, that he might be the firstborn among many brothers and sisters.

(Romans 8:29)

Enemy of progress!

One night a few months after we planted Musaale church, I saw in a dream, the devil was setting up sharp arrows pointed at the church, ready for battle. In the dream, it was clear those arrows were meant to take me out. Now you know why Paul says.

"Taking the shield of faith with which you will be able to quench the fiery darts of the devil."

(Ephesians 6:16)

The setup looked like the army formations we see in ancient war movies like Braveheart, King Arthur or the Gladiator.

That's when it dawned on me how serious my calling to plant a church in my hometown was and the spiritual impact it would have on people's lives. The devil never attacks anyone that is not a threat to the kingdom of darkness. Resistance is not meant to defeat us, but to reveal us. To challenge us to be stronger and to build even more strength to keep going. I have come to the conclusion, a theory in my own understanding and experience, and these are my thoughts; God uses the devil to strengthen us. While the devil is bent on destroying us and our purpose with arrows of resistance and destruction, God uses them to strengthen us so we can do even more for the Kingdom as we grow through overcoming resistance. When you face resistance as you sincerely pursue God's call on your life, you might think it to be some sort of punishment because it is often very personal. You may think this when people are leaving you, money is running out, or you have a persistent ailment.

I had known that Christianity was war and that following Jesus was war. I had read other people's stories on spiritual warfare, but now I was facing it. I was in the middle of it. I knew that we needed to be a church of prayer and I needed to be a man of prayer if I was going to stand the resistance. You see, the enemy will wage war on the church by waging war on you. He wants to discredit and discourage your ministry effort, so you give up and let the church die. The devil knows that when the church grows, when more people come to the saving knowledge of Jesus Christ, he loses control, he loses territory. Serving your purpose in Christ will not be a walk in the park. It will get down and dirty and messy; it is war! You do not take over territory without a fight. Oh, but the joy of victory when you see God place the devil in his rightful place under your feet after you have done all and stood.

> *Finally, be strong in the Lord and in his mighty power. Put on the full armor of God, so that you can take your stand against the devil's schemes. For our struggle is not against flesh and blood, but against the rulers, against the authorities, against the powers of this dark world and against the spiritual forces of evil in the heavenly realms. Therefore put on the full armor of God, so that when the day of evil comes, you may be able to stand your ground, and after you have done everything, to stand. Stand firm then, with the belt of truth buckled around your waist, with the breastplate of righteousness in place, and with your feet fitted with the readiness that comes from the gospel of peace. In addition to all this, take up the shield of faith, with which you can extinguish all the flaming arrows of the evil one. Take the helmet of salvation and the sword of the Spirit, which is the word of God.*

> **(Ephesians 6:10-17)**

The devil will fight your efforts to live out your calling on many fronts because he knows the eternal implications it will have on people and for you. You will get to the point you say to God; I did not ask for this! The devil will undermine your ministry by false accusation. The Bible calls him the accuser of the brethren. People who have never met you will talk about you like they grew up in the same house as you. Some will do it with malicious intent, others will just talk as if they know you, but you don't want someone with questionable character to claim to be your good friend. The devil will use anything and anyone to undermine your reputation so as to discredit your ministry. God uses people, so does the devil. Sometimes the enemy will use people in your inner circle who claim to be with you, but really undermine you behind your back. Such people sow dissension and division and lead astray those who really want to learn and grow. Do not tolerate divisive people on your team. Talk to them, warn them and when there's no change, release them from your realm. This is why when God says to let people go. I let them go. No matter how important you think they are to your ministry, no matter how talented they are, divisive people are under the influence of the devil and have to be dealt with accordingly or they will hinder your effectiveness greatly unless they change.

After Moses had miraculously crossed the Red Sea, turned bitter water sweet, gotten Israel water from a rock and bread from Heaven, he faced a divisive spirit from Korah, Dathan, Abiram and 250 other men who were community leaders, members of the council.

They came as a group to oppose Moses and Aaron and said to them, "You have gone too far! The whole community is holy, every one of them, and the Lord is with them. Why do you set yourselves above the Lord's assembly?"

(Numbers 16:3)

The devil attacks your calling on all fronts, from within and from without. Sometimes it is subtle and seems legitimate, like in the case of what these guys said to Moses. Surely God loves everybody - true. Surely God can use anyone - true. Surely there is no monopoly on God and He speaks to everyone who listens to Him - true. Moses did what everyone of us who desires to see the Kingdom come should do; He took it to God. No arguments and self-defense; let God prove us. The devil wants to reduce your ministry to politics and opinions and arguments and strife, and you should not allow that. You owe it to yourself not to. Take every argument to God and through God and it will be settled adequately and thoroughly. Do not let anyone make light of God's calling on your life. Do not let them compare you to others either. If you allow it, it will undermine your impact. Your calling is special. It is as unique as you are. The devil will take you out if you defend yourself in arguments. He always wins when on his terms. But when you give Him Jesus, the devil is always thoroughly and eternally defeated.

When Moses heard this, he fell face down. Then he said to Korah and all his followers: In the morning, the Lord will show who belongs to Him and who is holy, and He will make that person come near Him.

(Numbers 16:4)

I said to my team, everyone is important, but no one is indispensable. The only person indispensable in this ministry is Jesus Himself. He can do without me, but I cannot do without Him. But, Jesus and I can do without you if you are not living right with Him. I appreciate everyone's effort, but you have to know who your real boss is. He watches your secret life and your public life. The moment He says you must step down, I will not hesitate to let you go. When I have asked people to step down from active ministry, I have asked them to stay in the church and learn and grow and worship if they know that this is where they want to be. Some have stayed, some have gone out and cursed me out. This is how you quickly start to realize who was genuinely involved with you and who was just along for the ride and the benefits.

The devil is persistent. He will use anyone he can find. His goal is to discourage you and wear you down through whatever means possible to the point you give up on your mission. But God is a constant friend, always there with you, fighting with you, fighting for you, helping you, defending you. As long as you stay your post and don't let go, God will build His church and you will always come out victorious. The key thing is to keep the main thing the main thing. The enemy will do anything to get you to lose focus. To get you to waste energy and time defending yourself against his false accusations instead of focusing on your mission. The truth is, in every two people against you, God will have 20 that are for you and with you. If you are not careful, you will waste your time on the two and fail to build and equip the 20. The enemy will seek to defeat you by distraction. Do not buy into it. Keep the main thing, the main thing. We have to remember God is sovereign. He is in charge. But there is value in the testing we face; God allows it. I have had the thought; why wouldn't God just tie the devil up and burn him, but that time is set and it will come. In the meantime, we stand, we grow, we persist in faith. If we withstand the testing and pass, we can be entrusted with more in the Kingdom of our God.

After several years of our church's existence, I had another dream one night and this time, the devil was carrying his arrows and war platform and leaving. By now, people were genuinely coming to Jesus. The church was growing organically. I say organically because strength was being built one person at a time. Discipleship is a one by one, on one thing. Many people were witnessing Christianity played out before their eyes in ways they had never seen before. They had been looking for a real practical experience and I'm glad they found it in our church. The world is looking for a church that will be what we say we are. We ought to lead by example at home, at school, at the office, at the games, at church, we ought to be the same person everywhere, not just when we want to make an impression. Our yes ought to be yes and our no ought to be no, and the world ought to see that. We must be a church the devil will accuse, but when the people who heard the accusations meet you, they will wonder what the accuser was on about because they don't see any truth in what they heard out there. I'm in no way talking about a perfect church. There is no such church. I'm talking about an excellent church. It consists of imperfect, broken people giving their best, serving a perfect, loving and gracious God who is continually perfecting His bride, the church.

Loving people!

I mentioned earlier that as the church started to grow, God started to bring about a shaking, a sifting to get rid of the superficial. God calls us to love people and He said to me when we planted the church, just love people the best you can son; leave the growth of the church up to ME.

One of the mistakes we tend to make as leaders is to choose favorites. There are definitely people we naturally connect with more easily, but when leading a church, you must make an effort to connect with everyone impartially. Don't pick and choose. God will eventually start to separate the wheat from the chaff and you will know who God approves to work with at a higher level and entrust with responsibility, and who not to, but you just keep loving everyone.

Love must be sincere. Hate what is evil; cling to what is good.

(Romans 12:9)

When God started to ask me to confront people and let them go, I reasoned with Him saying, where is the love in that God? You asked me to love people, right? On top of that, people started to question the church slogan, *"Changing the world with the love of Jesus."*

They asked, Where is the love he keeps talking about?

The answer was in the scripture I just shared. You see, people want to be loved their own way and there is no such love in the Kingdom. The church ought to love people God's way or it's not the love of God and is not representing God. If you love people their way, you might just be a social club. Confronting people for deliberately living compromising lifestyle choices that are not a good representation of Christ is not loving them any less. The scripture says, "Love sincerely, but hate evil, cling to what is good."

If you entertain and rationalize anything that dishonors God in the name of love and yet you are aware of it, you are giving the devil a ride in your life and ministry. If you start to define love according to worldly standards, you have become an accomplice to the destruction of divine purpose in your life. The enemy's goal is to sideline you with counterfeit love and takeover. Nothing is more dangerous to the church than embracing counterfeit love. It looks like they are serving God on the surface, but actually serves the prince of darkness. Biblical love calls men to account. It calls men to repentance from things the Bible does not condone. You cannot use the Bible to justify any action as love that undermines God's purpose because the very Bible will call you out.

"Those whom I love I rebuke and discipline. So be earnest and repent."

(Revelations 3:19)

We confront people when God leads us to because we love them, because God loves them, because the health and authenticity of our ministry depends on it, because the fulfillment of their God-ordained destiny depends on it. God confronts to heal, to correct, to set what is upside down right side up. We confront people about the issues in their lives not to judge them, but to love them like God does.

So, confront, confront, confront however uncomfortable it feels. And if they walk away from you for that, you did your part. Leave it all to God.

The future God has for us is waiting on the other side of the things we are willing to confront. Not everyone I have confronted for correction has taken it well. But those who have taken it well have become fruitful individuals wherever they have gone and those who stayed have become an asset to the ministry. This is why God can ask me to leave the church in their hands.

Here is another scripture on why confronting wrong character and wrong motives on your team is not judgmental, but actually sincerely loving people.

And have you completely forgotten this word of encouragement that addresses you as a father addresses his son? It says, "My son, do not make light of the Lord's discipline, and do not lose heart when he rebukes you, because the Lord disciplines the one he loves, and he chastens everyone he accepts as his son." Endure hardship as discipline; God is treating you as his children. For what children are not disciplined by their father? If you are not disciplined—and everyone undergoes discipline— then you are not legitimate, not true sons and daughters at all. Moreover, we have all had human fathers who disciplined us and we respected them for it. How much more should we submit to the Father of spirits and live!

They disciplined us for a little while as they thought best, but God disciplines us for our good, in order that we may share in his holiness. No discipline seems pleasant at the time, but painful. Later on, however, it produces a harvest of righteousness and peace for those who have been trained by it. Therefore, strengthen your feeble arms and weak knees. "Make level paths for your feet," so that the lame may not be disabled, but rather healed.

(Hebrews 12:5-13)

God loves you too much to let you get away with what will lead you down a self-destructive path. God knows how to intervene in each of our lives and we do ourselves a huge favor when we respond to the correction instead of continuing our own way. You cannot be fruitful for the Kingdom if you do not submit to God's correction in your life. When God started to corner me and bring about realignment through correction and discipline, I'm glad I said yes! I don't think I would be a pastor if I did not. I do not think I would have had all the ministry experiences I have so far had if I did not respond to God's correction. God teaches us, rebukes us, corrects us, disciplines us before He uses us. You cannot give what you do not have. We become God's correction officers once we have passed through the correction process ourselves. Pastors and church leaders are God's police! But a policeman who has not been trained will mishandle and abuse the job. I'm not talking about theological training here. I'm talking about a spiritual experience with the living God that changes you from the inside out and teaches you God's heart for the world. If we hurry to make corrections in others when we ourselves have not submitted to correction, we will be like the sons of Sceva in Acts 19. The demons beat them and ate their lunch.

"You cannot give what you do not have."

Chapter 8

Vision Made Clear

"Write the vision and make it plain on tablets, That he may run who reads it. For the vision is yet for an appointed time; But at the end it will speak, and it will not lie. Though it tarries, wait for it; Because it will surely come, It will not tarry.

(Habakkuk 2:2-3)

I used to think that building large church buildings, creating great worship music for the global church to sing and becoming like some of the churches I had been to and seen was the vision I needed to have for our church. In fact, for a long time, I wanted to pastor a church that looked like Hillsong church. I still do, but in a different light, as I am going to share with you in this chapter. I was inspired to want to plant a church at a Hillsong conference in Sydney, Australia, when I saw more than twenty thousand people gathered in worship at the Acer Arena. I said, "God, You are no respecter of persons. You can do this in the most happening place, a.k.a Mbale in eastern Uganda too. You can help me create a place where thousands gather from around the world for the purpose of extending the Kingdom to the ends of the earth."

I loved the atmosphere of expectancy and faith and rawness they had created at Hillsong Church and wanted the church that I pastor to look like that. Watoto church, the church I started my journey with Jesus at, is a great and big church too and I partly wanted to pastor a church that looked like it. Most of my work ethic was influenced by Watoto.

One night in a dream/vision, I was standing on a hill. The surrounding area looked like Israel. At a distance, I could see what looked like the temple mount in Jerusalem with the sun shining brightly on it. I could see on one side in a valley there was Hillsong church and the stage lights were switched off. On another side of the valley was Watoto Church and the stage lights were switched off too. I heard a voice say about the sun-lit golden dome, "That is the Macedonian church." The message I received was, "That is the kind of church I want you to be like, with the SON shining bright." When I woke up, I looked up the Macedonian Church and came to this portion of scripture.

And now, brothers and sisters, we want you to know about the grace that God has given the Macedonian churches. In the midst of a very severe trial, their overflowing joy and their extreme poverty welled up in rich generosity. For I testify that they gave as much as they were able, and even beyond their ability. Entirely on their own, they urgently pleaded with us for the privilege of sharing in this service to the Lord's people.

And they exceeded our expectations: They gave themselves first of all to the Lord, and then by the will of God also to us.

(2 Corinthians 8:1-5)

God had given me a blueprint for the kind of church we are called to be and would model after. You see, we can replicate what we see another church doing; Programs, songs, styles and even sermons, but we cannot replicate character that is born through adversity. God is looking for a church, a people who will model their ministry life after the biblical model, not the model of another church. Don't get me wrong; we ought to learn from others, the Bible says.

"As iron sharpens iron, so one person sharpens another"

(Proverbs 27:17).

We need to learn from each other, but when it comes to the heart of our ministry, our person, who we are called to be, we cannot learn that from someone else. The school of theology cannot teach you how to be the person God uniquely wants you to be. This is born from within us, through the experiences we grow through, and the grace we receive for those experiences. We become the person God uniquely designed us to be out of the pain we endure, the discouragement we persevere through, the trials we overcome with God's help. God knows how to create the right circumstances that bring out the character He knows will help us become effective in ministry. This is why you should not run for help to friends every time you have trouble. The first person to run to for help should always be God.

> God our refuge and strength; An ever-present help in trouble.
>
> **(Psalms 46:1).**

God is closer to us than anyone or anything else and He wants us to know that and consider Him over everyone and everything else. Knowing this is and making it key in our lives shapes the DNA of our ministry life.

God will often give you help through someone if that is what is needed. Most times, He will strengthen you for the process you have to go through. I have faced my own fair share of trials financially and physically over long periods. In fact, I'm going through an extensive period of financial trial as I write this book. I rarely get sick, and I mean, I do not get as much as a cold easily. In fact, I cannot remember when I last had one and I do not hope to have one in the future. The life-giving presence of Jesus sustains me. *"The power of life and death is in the tongue" (Proverbs 18:21).* Be careful what you speak over yourself.

When we planted Musaale church in 2014, I developed a cold/flu out of nowhere and like always, I rebuked it, refused it, took some hot honey and lemon to cut it off, but this one persisted. It stayed on for a while and continued for weeks. It developed into a painful cough and no matter what medication I took, it persisted. I prayed it away, spoke it away, but it stayed. Some scientific folks will say, well, you did not get the right medication. I want to tell you that science cannot short circuit a trial God has allowed that is meant to build inner strength and tenacity. No amount of money in all the world can short circuit a process God has ordained to build strength of character that enables us to serve Kingdom purposes effectively. Now you can try to run away from the process like Jonah. You can give up trying to move forward and make excuses that may sound justifiable in your eyes and in the eyes of observers. Job's wife would have understood if he gave up. In fact, she advised him to give up and die.

> His wife said to him, "Are you still maintaining your integrity? Curse God and die!"

(Job 2:9)

If Job had listened to his wife, we would only read two chapters about him today. He would be an example of how not to face a trial. But because Job persisted in faith, believing God, we read a lot more about his life as an example to learn from. God wants to help you write your story through the trials you face. How we persevere through our trials will help others coming behind us relate and keep going in their own trials. The examples we see about others help us realize we are not weirdos. Our own trials and how we overcome them is so that those who come after us will look and say, "If they could overcome this, then surely it is possible to overcome this" The people you lead will learn to cope through trial by how they see you handle trials. If a leader handles difficulty by complaining, blaming and grumbling, the people who serve under them will do the same. You have no right as a leader, pastor, teacher, parent, or big brother to demand a standard you do not exemplify.

Do everything without complaining or arguing, so that you may become blameless and pure, children of God without fault in a crooked and depraved generation, in which you shine like stars in the universe as you hold out the word of life.

(Philippians 2:14-16)

The overarching vision of the Church of Jesus Christ is to model the character of Jesus Christ to the world. To exemplify, to demonstrate, to show, to prove that Jesus is alive because He lives in us and the evidence is undeniable because the world can see Him in us. You cannot copy and paste this. This is not behavior modification or outward display of piety. This is inside out. It is not a position, but a disposition, an alignment, indwelling, embodying. What we embody becomes what we give out to the world. Buildings, infrastructure, audio visual equipment and all the technology we use are simply tools to help us continue to demonstrate, exemplify and multiply Jesus' experiences, nothing more.

The grass withers and the flowers fall, but the word of our God endures forever."

(Isaiah 40:8)

145

I have often said to my leadership team at Musaale Church, the songs we sing and the messages we preach are not the core of what our church is about. We must prepare the right songs, we must adequately prepare our messages, but they are simply a means to an end. The end is that the world will know Jesus is alive! God can show up and interrupt our songs, our sermons and programs all He wants any time He wants to. We want that everything we do will fall in line with who He wants us to be as a church where we are. This does not mean that we have no program. We are very programmed, actually, but we do not depend on the program. We want to depend on the leading of the Holy Spirit and this is not born on stage. It is born in private. If you cannot hear from God in private, if you cannot recognize His voice in your private life, you will not recognize His now word for someone on a stage. The stage does not make the moment, we do and if His presence is not cultivated in us, we waste the stage moment. The trials we face with God will help us cultivate an intimacy with God that will enable us to recognize His voice and His ways. His presence in us is the power to change the world.

> They went out and preached everywhere, and the Lord worked through them, confirming His word by the signs that accompanied it.

(Mark 16:10)

Many people ask if God still performs miracles like He did in the Bible when Jesus was here on earth. I want to tell you that He does. God has not changed how He works. The vision of the church of Jesus Christ is to allow His presence to so invade the house because, in His presence, there will be signs, manifestations and wonders. You cannot fake this. You are either in submission and surrender to allowing the presence of God precedence over your life and church or you are not. You cannot witness the signs and wonders of God without sincerely sold-out, submitted lives that are being continually strengthened through trial and suffering.

God wants that the uniqueness He placed within you becomes one of His expressions to the world, not a replica of something else. Replicating is easy. Uniqueness, on the other hand, is hard work that involves going through pain and hardship, failure and some mockery. Discovering your uniqueness as a pastor, a church leader, is a journey to be invested in, not a class to attend. God hopes you will make every effort to get on the journey and embrace all the discomfort and inconvenience that comes with it because the lessons therein are pertinent to your calling. There are things we use from Hillsong Church like Discovery Class, a short foundation course for new converts or some who have been in the church for a long time but still got questions because they never had a proper foundation in the Christian faith. Some things are across the board and there is no need to re-invent the wheel because scripture is scripture. We can learn from others, but we cannot build our Kingdom vision/dream on someone else's sweat.

The Macedonian church

Back to the Macedonia church, the scripture says; They went through severe trial but overflowed with joy. They went through severe poverty, but overflowed with generosity. They gave themselves fully, first to God and then to the ministry.

God had given me a model for the kind of church He wanted.

God was saying, I want a church that will follow me wholeheartedly. Not only when things are going according to plan, but even when you feel like I have abandoned you. A church that will continue to be generous, helping others and not looking to their own interests in the tough times. A church that will allow the goodness of God to flow freely and continually no matter the season. This is the kind of church I intend to be and to lead. Where we do not act kindly because we feel kind, but even when we do not. Where we are generous not only when we have plenty to go around, but even when we ourselves are in need.

I have since learned that generosity is not a matter of what you have. It is a matter of your being. If you are a generous person, you will be generous no matter what you are going through. And if you are mean, it doesn't matter how much you have or do not have.

I have also learned that the church of Jesus Christ is supposed to be the happiest place on earth. That our joy is not to be derived from external circumstances, it is not derived from what God does or does not do, but who He is to us and in us. Our joy is an overflow of our fixation with the person of Jesus Christ and the working of the Holy Spirit and that joy is the strength of the church. The joy of the Lord is our strength.

I said earlier that when we planted Musaale church, I had enough funds to support the church, to pay bills for a while. Eventually, my business started to suffer drought. I must tell you, when we started the church and I invested all the money to get it going and running, I thought in my mind that God was going to bless my business tremendously and I was going to overflow in blessings like never before. The opposite of that became true. Business started to dwindle, and dwindle, and pick up and dwindle, and dwindle some more until the taps completely dried out. The challenge to be like the Macedonian church, overflowing with joy in the midst of severe trial, was now in play. I wish I could say that I responded perfectly well, but no, I did not. I complained to God and I lamented. I felt abandoned. I felt betrayed by God, but I stayed the course, continued making sure we had services happening every weekend and required payments were being made. I made sure to show up and preach an encouraging sermon to the congregation even when I was fighting back tears the morning before I came to the church meeting venue because I did not understand what was going on.

We started defaulting on payments and I had to explain to our landlords that we would be coming around with the payments and somehow we did, and then we defaulted and descended into debt.

I have found that God will never give you a word He does not intend to fulfill in your life. Many people cling to the promises and claim them, but severe trial is also a portion of scripture we must embrace along with God's good promises.

Holding on to the promises helps us cope in the midst of the trials. I cannot say that I like the severe trials part. But, the lessons, the strength, the character growth, I would not trade the trials for anything. I have grown leaps and bounds through my trials than I ever have through my mountain top experiences.

The people you lead watch how you handle trying times and that can be a building or breaking moment for your church. I said earlier that I wish I could say I responded well. I said that I complained and lamented, felt betrayed and abandoned. This was between God and me. I make sure my team never sees me complaining or grumbling or being negative in any way about what I think God is doing or not doing. The last thing you want is for your church to be filled with grumblers and complainers. You set that example. Besides, we are trying to be like the biblical Macedonian church. Many on my church team reading this will be surprised that I have even had these emotions in private. Take your issues and feelings about your circumstances to God always as your first and your last source.

As I write this book, there are a lot of things I still do not understand about God and why He allows certain things to drag on in our lives for a long time even when we have prayed and fasted over them again and again, been faithful. One thing I'm daily learning to do is live without a grudge against God or people and to fear no evil. To trust that His plans are good and what is happening now will pass after certain intended purposes are fulfilled even though I may not fully grasp what those purposes are right now, and the answers still look so distant.

Chapter 9

Chasing Dreams!

I don't know about you, but I'm a dreamer. Not a daydreamer, but a believer. I believe that anything is possible when we trust God and do our best! I have often found that in me exist two conflicting persons though; One who believes all things are absolutely possible all the time, and the other who periodically questions that position. I like the former to win rather than the latter. Sometimes, I will stand up and boldly declare what I believe God is going to do. I'm convinced of it. Then I will go back to the house and lay down on the floor, wondering how exactly this will happen. Like Joseph, dreams come to me when I'm asleep. I also have wild imaginations of possibilities in my waking life. I have often dreamed of flying into space without using a rocket. God would take me there. I have since had many dreams/visions of myself as an astronaut in space or at the international space center floating around like one of those in charge of keeping the earth's communications wheel going. I'm not joking. I have had these dreams many times, some a few months ago. These are phenomenal dreams to have actually! If you do not dream, I feel for you. You are missing out on a whole other world, lol! Sometimes in my dreams, I'll be taking off in a rocket into space. Other times, I will be returning and successfully landing after my mission in space is complete. Sometimes, I have dreamed of my rocket crashing to pieces on return to earth. Not good! The crash usually happens when I spent the day worried or very concerned about something.

Once a few years ago, I had an out-of-body experience where I left earth, not as an astronaut but just as I am. I was taken through an ascending dark corridor that emerged into very beautiful golden and blue colored formations of lights in space. It did not last long, unfortunately, even though I wanted to stay longer. I have since had other dreams where I was standing in a glorious glass building in what was like Heaven and looking at the Nebula in its magnificent colors. I have had some amazing dreams in my sleep, I tell you. Again, if you do not dream when you sleep, call me. You are missing out...

If you do not remember your dreams, start to practice taking note of your night dreams because God is talking to you about possibilities, wanting to build your imagination and giving you messages on the future and on people and things in your life. Dreams are often God's conversations with us that are meant to cause us to seek out to know more. As we do, we are continuing the conversation. Sound good? You have no idea! There is nothing like a conversation with the divine. God is always talking to us. It's just that many are not paying attention.

When I was about to finish my 2-year college diploma/associate's degrees in 2001, I had a dream that felt so real that when I woke up, I was so disappointed. In this dream, I was at the airport on my way to the United Kingdom. I met someone I did not recognize who asked where I was going and I said to him I was on my way to London. I then proceeded to board a British Airways Boeing 747 aircraft for my flight. It all sounded so real and felt so real that when I woke up, I cannot tell you just how disappointed I was. I did not have a passport at the time and had no plans to get one. There was no way at the time I could afford a trip to London, not to mention passport fees. Fast forward January 2003, I had a strong gut feeling inside me that it was time for that dream from 2001 to become a reality.

I jokingly said to someone, "I'm going to London this year." They responded with mocking laughter, saying I did not even have a passport. They were right, I did not have a passport, no connections, but I had a prompting inside that felt so real, I had to speak it out. Do not look down on the dreams and promptings you receive. God is speaking to you. Speak life over yourself and your future. It is not wishful thinking if you are being prompted by the Spirit from inside and are a dedicated, faithful person. In the month of March 2003, I received a phone call from my supervisor at the children's church where I was volunteering. They said the Watoto choir was looking for a chaperone/singer to join their team for a tour that was starting August the same year. Long story short, I joined the choir, got my first passport and was on a British Airways flight to, you guessed it, London, and have been traveling the world ever since.

Here's how it all happened; I received a dream in 2001, was disappointed it was just a dream even though it felt so real. I believed it was a preamble of things to come, did not know when or how it would happen. My circumstances could not make sense of it. I joined children's church later the same year as a volunteer. I gave my all as a volunteer, which got my supervisor's attention. I was not in it to impress anyone. Doing things right, showing up on time for things was a principle at work in my life. One of the good things I inherited from my parents was to show up on time and not to be lazy. My supervisor recommended me to join the Watoto choir, God used him as a conduit on my life's journey, but it was my faithful dedication to serving that drew his attention to me. Just because God gave you a dream does not mean you sit back and wait for it to take effect. It will never happen that way. The Bible says about Joseph, he had dreams, was sold into slavery, but everywhere Joseph went as a slave, he carried himself with an excellent spirit that those who supervised him noticed him as a class apart and placed him in charge of things.

Unless you change and become like little children, you will never enter the kingdom of heaven.

(Matthew 18:3)

Children have an unlimited imagination. There are no boundaries to the things children can possibly think up as possible. The Bible says.

Nothing will be impossible with our God for those who believe.

(Mark 9:23)

To be like children from God's point of view is to look at life with unlimited imagination in regard to dreams, potential and possibilities. It is to have this innocent expectation that God means you well and He wants to do you good, even when you have faced some painful disappointments in life. To continue to be childlike takes intentional effort and work because life will do everything possible to make us "realist" adults who have no imagination. This does not mean to live in denial of reality, but it is to keep a pure, innocent and unadulterated view of God. A God who is not limited to or subject to the laws of science and nature. God exists in the unlimited, unstoppable, unending wide-open spaces of faith and invites us to live there. I guess that's why I keep going into space in my dreams.

When it comes to faith, we must never grow up! Now I'm in no way advocating for childishness. The Bible does not say to be childish, but to be childlike; there's a difference. The Bible calls us to give up irresponsible, childish ways. But when it comes to our faith in God, the Bible says to be like children with an unlimited imagination.

The dreams we have at night are our conversations with God. He communicates to us about our waking life actions and decisions and their consequences and how we can alter our course of action to bring about a divine outcome even in the seemingly small details of life.

God also uses dreams to bring us into the realms of the impossible becoming possible. I have accomplished everything in my night dreams. I have gotten married to the girl of my dreams, flown a plane, flown a helicopter, taken charge of a rocket, spent time in space, stood on top of mountains, stood on top of the Empire state building. I have also flown without wings. I have had some nightmares too that have spoken to and altered my waking life actions and saved me from making stupid decisions.

I have always been a dreamer. I mean, when you do not like the reality you are born in, dreaming is like an escape. I, later on, found out in the Bible that thinking on good things is not an escape. It is thinking in line with God because God is good and wants to bring us into that place of experiencing His goodness. In fact, the Bible encourages us to think on the good things of God, to expect them and continue to anticipate them even when we face negative circumstances. It takes work! It is spiritual warfare. Many people talk negative talk, but expect a positive outcome out of life. They say negative things about their children but are disappointed when their children fall short of some of life's expectations. You will reap a harvest from the words of your mouth. If you have children, bless them every morning and encourage their imagination.

And the Lord spoke to Moses, saying, speak to Aaron and his sons, saying, This is the way you shall bless the children of Israel. Say to them,

> The Lord bless you and keep you; The Lord make His face shine upon you, And be gracious to you. The Lord lift up His countenance upon you and give you

peace. *So they shall put my name on the children of Israel and I will bless them.*

(Numbers 6:22-27)

Jesus was a dreamer! This is why the establishment of His time did not like Him. He showed up with a dream to alter the direction of humanity forever and the pharisees and high priests thought this was another crazy guy, a carpenter's son from Nazareth making big, larger than life, unachievable, even blasphemous claims. Dreamers often seem crazy to the world until what they say becomes reality. In the words of Nelson Mandela, *"It always seems impossible until it's done!"*

"The spirit of the sovereign Lord is upon me to preach the gospel to the poor. He has sent me to heal the brokenhearted, to proclaim liberty to the captives and recovery of sight to the blind. To set at liberty those who are oppressed; To proclaim the acceptable year of the Lord."

(Luke 4:18-19)

Jesus was saying, I have come to change the world! I have come here to alter the destiny of humanity, to set men free, give blind people sight. The only problem is Jesus was from a place they all knew and from parents they all knew. He had not been to seminary or school of theology and He claimed to know God. How dare He? They took offense at Him for his seemingly preposterous claims to be any better than He could really be, even more powerful than the high priests and the preachers of the time who did not talk like that or preach like that. They were 'humble' and 'unassuming' folks. They thought Jesus was being presumptuously arrogant to think He was any different or better them, scholars and teachers of the law. Truthfully, they were dry on religion. Jesus was God become man to rescue men and demonstrate to men how life ought to be done. He may have been born in the most ordinary fashion, but it was so He could identify with those He came to save. He was still fully God and yet fully man. Jesus spoke with such authority and confidence and the religious, adult folk of his time did not like that. God wants us to be confidently assured that what He promised He will do. He wants that we will receive His word as children, speak it out, declare it until we see the manifestation of it. Speaking things that are not as if they already are till they become is the way of faith, not wishful thinking. If you truly believe God and are invested in becoming the person God wants you to be, childlike faith is the way.

When we planted Musaale church, I was a first-generation pastor, I had ministry experience as a children's church facilitator, as a team leader/pastor leading a team around the world, as a worship leader in a mega church of more than 30,000, but I had not been to Bible school, I wasn't sure I was qualified to plant a church. All I had was this dream, this passion, this calling deep inside to create a place where people encountered the living, life-transforming Jesus I had encountered. When I spoke of what I intended to do, some said it would not work. I was making a mistake. I believed God would do something to prove Himself and His calling on my life, so I gave it everything. Over the years, we have witnessed people getting healed, people meeting Jesus for the first time and making life-altering decisions and the church has grown to 350 people meeting in two locations. Now we are still a far off from where I would like Musaale Church to go. One day, I would like to see 40% or more of the population of Mbale and Soroti towns where we are now become members of our church. I dream of building large state-of-the-art auditoriums that will accommodate thousands at a time in the multiple Jesus celebrations we will put on every weekend. I'm in America now chasing dreams to plant a life-giving church to continue the mission God has placed on my life. I will spend the rest of my days planting life-giving churches wherever God calls me in this good earth He created.

Speak life!

Jesus spoke of His own resurrection before it happened.

'Destroy this temple and I will raise it in three days!

- Jesus (John 2:19)

The pharisees argued with Him; "It took our ancestors decades to build this thing. Who do you think you are man?" Get out of here, you presumptuous, blasphemous fellow! Fast forward about two years or so years later at the grave site where Jesus was buried on the third day after His death on the cross.

He is not here; he has risen, just as he said. Come and see the place where he lay.

(Matthew 28:6)

He is risen just like He what? Like He said! If the son of God had to speak forth His own resurrection, then what about us sons of men? God wants that our speech and our proclamations about life, about the future will come into agreement with His word. We must keep the childlike innocence that receives God's grace and promises without argument like Mary.

"Be it unto me according to your word."

(Luke 1:38)

There is no other standard by which God establishes His plans in our lives other than the truth of His word. We must speak faith-filled words because that is what God is watching for to perform and fulfill in our generation.

God is watching over His word to perform it.

(Jeremiah 1:12)

Joseph was a dreamer! His brothers were not so happy with all his dreaming. They already hated him as it was because his father loved him and favored him over all his other sons. And now, for Joseph to think he would have all these dreams threatened everything. They challenged him, rubbished his dreams the best they could. "We are desert folk man, livestock herders. We do not do that kind of stuff man, forget all these silly ambitions of yours. Do not let Daddy's love get to your head man, do not be so proud as to think you can be so much."

Joseph is a type of Old Testament Christ looking at how God used his dreams to save the nation of Israel. Christ would be the ultimate Savior of the nation of Israel and all of humanity. Every dream God gives us is going to be way bigger than us. It will look unachievable. It is meant to fulfill a divine purpose, the saving of many lives. If your dreams are all about you and what you want out of life, then they are not from God. Our dreams will benefit us, but God does not waste a dream on selfish pursuits

The establishment of Christ's time killed Him for his bold claims. They were offended that He would dare talk like He did. The Pharisees were kind of like Joseph's brothers.

When people know you, when they know your family background, dreaming about doing great things that have never been seen can present some complications in relationships.

What good can come from Nazareth? What angered most people about Jesus' claims about God being His DAD and what He wanted to accomplish for humanity is that they knew His village and His family. Many people are happy with you keeping the status quo, not rocking the boat, not trying to change your history. Many people have embraced life as they found it or as it found them. God brought us here to change the world, not to maintain the status quo. God expects that in our generation, we will do something that will challenge the next to do even better. Something that will outlast us and echo into eternity.

"Isn't this the carpenter's son? Isn't his mother's name Mary, and aren't his brothers James, Joseph, Simon and Judas? Aren't all his sisters with us? Where then did this man get all these things?" And

they took offense at him. But Jesus said to them, "A prophet is not without honor except in his own town and in his own home." And he did not do many miracles there because of their lack of faith.

(Matthew 13:55-58)

Don't let your background, what people know of you and think of you hinder you from dreaming big dreams. On the flip side, don't allow yourself to talk you out of dreaming big dreams. For a long time, I struggled with my own self-worth. Sometimes I have looked at my dreams and thought, who do you think you are?

Like I said before, my siblings and I dealt with our fair share of ridicule, embarrassment and shame growing up in poverty with an alcoholic earthly father. That stuff can get to you and make you have a victim mentality, get you to define your whole world around it and think the whole world is against you. A victim mentality will cause you to notice all the bad stuff around you in the midst of all the good things in life that far outweigh the negatives. I mentioned earlier that I was a people pleaser because I needed people to want me, to accept me. I fed off of their approval. I did not know my own value. It was really bad until Jesus started to help me deal with it saying, this is not going to work for you child. I died for you because you were valuable to God, to the Kingdom. God needs you. God wants you. God likes you and there is nothing you have to do for God to be for you. If God, the Boss of all things thinks you are something, that is something man. Freedom!

Somebody needs to pause and think on that for a little while. *"God needs you, God wants you, God likes you and there is nothing you have to do for God to be for you."*

Drink it in and let it heal you. It took me a while to start really believing this about myself and allowing it to become my reality. God knows I'm still making an effort to internalize this truth. Walking by faith, experiencing uncertain circumstances that bring pain and suffering will sometimes cause me to feel those emotions of inadequacy all over again because of the feelings of abandonment and neglect. It can feel like punishment. It is in those times that God reminds me of my value, of the greatness He placed inside of me, that my value is not attached to a thing, a feeling, an achievement, a status. My value is intrinsic and cannot be compromised in any way. Joseph had to learn his true value by suffering through the unfair things he faced. He was trained by his trials to prioritize and later live the dream by the circumstances he grew through.

When God lets us dreamers walk in the wilderness, it may feel like the dream is dead when you are in the midst of it, but actually it is where the dream is refined. He is winning us of attachments that will not serve the purposes of the dream. A lot of the attachments we are not usually aware of, the wilderness reveals them in us. God is winning us of false confidence, of deriving value and worth from material and temporary things. You see, it is easy to dream and profess undying love to God when everything is going well. Jesus' disciples did that, promising to die with Jesus if it was required. But the Bible says when that day came, they fled for the lives. They thought the dream was dead when Jesus was arrested and sentenced to death on a cross. Some of the circumstances we go through will make it look like our dream is dead and buried and impossible to fulfill. But the disciples up to this point reasoned from a human point of view.

They were about to be ushered into a whole new arena of divine, supernatural thinking where impossible things are absolutely possible, where dead people come back to life and change the world.

I have learned in my life as a dreamer that I'm often afraid of success more than I'm afraid of failure. I'm afraid of greatness, more than I'm afraid of mediocrity. In fact, it is easier to accept failure and mediocrity sometimes than it is to accept success and great achievement. It is easier to accept criticism than it is to accept a compliment. I've had a fair share of my own failures in relationships, in business deals etc. I have learned over the years that dreams are often tested and refined in the furnace of the failures and losses we suffer. They remind us of what truly matters, that this human form is for now, but what we do ought to exceed us and echo into eternity.

> "Our deepest fear is not that we are inadequate. Our deepest fear is that we are powerful beyond measure. It is our light, not our darkness that most frightens us. We ask ourselves, 'Who am I to be brilliant, gorgeous, talented, fabulous?' Actually, who are you not to be? You are a child of God. You're playing small does not serve the world. There is nothing enlightened about shrinking so that other people won't feel insecure around you. We are all meant to

shine, as children do. We were born to make manifest the glory of God that is within us. It's not just in some of us; it's in everyone.

And as we let our own light shine, we unconsciously give other people permission to do the same. As we are liberated from our own fear, our presence automatically liberates others."

— Marianne Williamson,

Chapter 10

The Price of Dreaming

A line in Michael Bolton's song from the early '80s titled, *"How Am I Supposed To Live Without You,"* goes, "I don't wanna know the price I'm gonna pay for dreaming." Jesus said everyone who wanted to be a dreamer like Him, who wanted to change the world, would have to pay a price. If you were not willing to pay the price for the dream, the dream would not be realized. You would be a daydreamer. Do you want to know the price you are going to pay for your dreams? Being in the middle of it at this point in my life, I don't. It is better to commit fully and simply trust God in faith because if you know, you may be too frightened to leave the shore.

> *Then Jesus said to His disciples, "Whoever wants to be my disciple must deny themselves and take up*

their cross and follow me.

(Matthew 16:24)

Must deny themselves! This means many things; Give up their rights, their comforts and conveniences, their priorities, their will and selfish pursuits.

Take up their cross! The cross was a symbol of suffering and pain and death. Jesus was saying if we wanted to change the world the way He did, we would have to voluntarily embrace a life that would be uncomfortable, inconvenient, painful, a life that would stretch us. We would have to embrace it fully to see the results that come with it. Taking up your cross is not making yourself suffer. It is not mechanical. The pain of carrying our cross happens as part of the calling. To try and create suffering in the pretext of carrying your cross is religious mumbo jumbo.

I thought I had lots of friends before I started to share my astronomical dreams out loud. When I said I was going to plant a church and all the things I had in my heart to accomplish, I lost friends. This was not surprising though, because I also felt deeply in my heart when I started to pursue my dreams (take up my cross and follow) that things would never be the same again. I knew that this was going to be the separator. I knew that I would no longer have anything in common with some of my friends at the time. Chasing dreams (carrying your cross) will bring you closer to God, but may alienate you from those you know because they won't be able to relate to your experiences. I do not know how many times I have wanted to share what was happening in my life with someone who could identify with me on my journey. To share my frustrations and challenges, but could not easily find anyone who could relate. When I tried to call my pastor, God would stop me saying, you got ME! We need people in our lives, but sometimes God wants us in a place where we are depending on Him and no other. It is important to discern this or you will find yourself depending on people for things only God can do for you and give you.

Dreaming can be lonely

Dreaming can be a lonely place, but God will always be there! If you are married though and chose a suitable partner, you have a confidant to share your dreams and struggles with or I think you should because marriage is meant for two people who support each other and spur each other on to accomplishing dreams. If you do not have such a marriage partner, and I'm talking man and woman in holy matrimony, then you can work towards making this happen. Everything takes work, especially in marriage.

I thought for a while that being a single pastor, and planting a church could not go together. When I heard other people say it or church members say it, I feared for myself. I feared that my church plant would be a flop. But then I remembered Jesus was a single guy, so was Paul, and they changed the world forever.

I'm going to get married at some point. God has made that clear. He has a pretty girl for me. But while I'm still single, I've got everything I need to make the dream work. When I marry that pretty girl, we will begin a new chapter of married's changing the world together. But right now, I'm fully representing the singles changing the world chapter. And all the singles said, AMEN!

When you share your frustrations with people who are not dreamers or who cannot connect with you at the level of your dreams, you will get even more frustrated. But I found that there is another dreamer who went before me. Who declared things in His lifetime and they became just as He said. A friend who sticks closer than a brother, His name is Jesus. Chasing dreams will draw you closer to Jesus like nothing can. It will bring you into a place where you have nothing else to hold on to but Jesus. When Jesus carried that cross to Golgotha, the hill on which he was crucified, it was a lonely place. There was no one in history who had walked in his shoes. His journey was unique, just as He was. Jesus can empathize with us, feel us, feel our pain and suffering because He went through all that and more, plus bought the t-shirt.

One who has unreliable friends soon comes to ruin,
but there is a friend who sticks closer than a brother.

(Proverbs 18:24)

Joseph had a dream, and when he told it to his brothers, who already hated him, they hated him all the more. Not everyone will give you a high five for dreaming and wanting to change the world.

"Listen to this dream I had: We were binding sheaves of grain out in the field when suddenly my sheaf rose and stood upright, while your sheaves gathered around mine and bowed down to it." His brothers said to him, "Do you intend to reign over us? Will

169

you actually rule us?" And they hated him all the more because of his dream and what he had said. Then he had another dream, and he told it to his brothers. "Listen," he said, "I had another dream, and this time the sun and moon and eleven stars were bowing down to me." When he told his father as well as his brothers, his father rebuked him and said, "What is this dream you had? Will your mother and I and your brothers actually come and bow down to the ground before you?" His brothers were jealous of him, but his father kept the matter in mind.

(Genesis 37:9-11)

It is very hard to convince others of the dreams God has placed in your heart because they won't be able to relate. They were not there when God spoke to you. It is unrealistic to expect them to clap their hands for you in celebration.

As someone once said; The fastest way to kill a dream is to tell it to people who do not believe you. Sometimes we want people to agree with us, to support us, but I have realized sometimes God will use people to disagree with us, even betray us and leave us because of our dreams. This because we will be motivated and directed to place all of our trust in the dream giver and not in people who have no power to make the dream happen. If the dream God has given us is going to happen, then the God of the dream must become our source and no other.

Rhythms of dreams

Everything God does in our lives runs on a rhythm and timing. When I quit my job at Watoto choir, I struggled financially for the first few months. Like I mentioned earlier, I had spent most of my savings on building a house for my parents.

I quit my job on God's leading to pursue the dreams He had placed in my heart. A few months into going after my dreams, I got an invitation to return to my job of touring the world. Was it tempting? Maybe a little, I was broke. It was more insulting than tempting to me at that point, to be honest. I had honorably served my time and honorably resigned from my job. The Bible says to owe no man anything except the continuing debt of love. As far as I was concerned, I owed nothing. Did I need money when I was invited back? Yes, I did. I was struggling financially. But at that time, chasing my dreams was more important than the convenience of having money. Your dream has to mean more to you than the inconvenience and discomfort of lacking money or you will be distracted and jump onto whatever good-looking opportunity is offered and never accomplish your dream. You have to pay the price of the dream by keeping to the rhythm of your dream.

In the same season when I had quit my job, someone else had offered to support me financially. They said to me before I quit my job; We know what it's like to have no income after you quit a job. Let us know your monthly expenses and we will be happy to send the money to you. This seemed like an offer from Heaven. I forgot about it though. But when I started to experience financial struggles, waking up and looking at the ceiling with no plan for the day, it all came back to me. I thought to contact them and say, "About that offer."

But God said, don't do it! I said, get behind me, Satan! You do not have in mind the things of God. But it was the voice of God, so I obliged. Many things God asks you to do will not make sense at the time He does ask. As you stay on the path of dreaming with God, you will eventually learn that God doesn't want anyone taking credit or you giving another credit that only belongs to Him. Some help will distract your attention from the true source of your purpose and calling. You must pay the price of the dreams of your life by staying in the rhythm even when it's uncomfortable.

> If the Lord had not been on our side, let Israel say, if the Lord had not been on our side when people attacked us, they would have swallowed us alive when their anger flared against us; the flood would have engulfed us, the torrent would have swept over us, the raging waters would have swept us away. Praise be to the Lord, who has not let us be torn by their teeth. We have escaped like a bird from the fowler's snare, the snare has been broken, and we have escaped. Our help is in the name of the Lord, the Maker of heaven and earth.

(Psalms 124)

The key lines in this portion of scripture are; If the Lord had not been on our side and Our help is in the name of the Lord, the Maker of heaven and earth.

God wants that your story will tell His-story. That your dreams will be His dreams, His way. Plus, God knows, if we start to rely on other people, we may end up turning them into some kind of god depending on them in ways we should only be depending on almighty God, thus limit our dreams. Have you made someone else your source and not God? Sometimes, paying the price for our dreams is saying no to what seems like offers from God to meet our needs. You need discernment to tell, plus you must be connected and hearing from God continually in a word, a dream, a prompting, God is always speaking and we must be listening in lest we are distracted by the provision.

Work the work

If you are not willing to give up everything and bear up under all things for the sake of the dreams God has placed in your heart, you are only daydreaming. You must pay the price.

Chasing dreams and making them happen is inconvenient, uncomfortable, can be painful, it will cost you everything. Like someone once said, ***"Nothing worth having comes easy."***

> *Jesus replied, "No one who puts a hand to the plow and looks back is fit for service in the kingdom of God."*

(Luke 9:62)

God wants to know how serious you are about the dreams He has placed in your heart. God won't make your dreams happen because you prayed and fasted a lot about them, but because you worked the work for the dream, took the risks the dreams demanded, gave up what needed giving up for the sake of the call. Many in the church are frustrated that God is not coming through for them, but God is frustrated that all they do is pray, fast and not make the right moves. God gave us brains for a reason. We are not robots!

Joshua is one character that amazes me in the Bible. God assured him of victory over his enemies, but Joshua still worked the work, did his best. Joshua paid the price.

> So Joshua marched up from Gilgal with his entire army, including all the best fighting men. The Lord said to Joshua, "Do not be afraid of them; I have given them into your hand. Not one of them will be able to withstand you."
>
> After an all-night march from Gilgal, Joshua took them by surprise. The Lord threw them into confusion before Israel, so Joshua and the Israelites defeated them completely at Gibeon. Israel pursued them along the road going up to Beth Horon and cut them down all the way to Azekah and Makkedah. As they fled before Israel on the road down from Beth Horon to Azekah, the Lord hurled large hailstones down on them, and more of them died from the hail than were killed by the swords of the Israelites.

(Joshua 10:7-11)

The gospel of name it and claim it is not the gospel of Jesus Christ. It is the deception of the enemy. It is witchcraft. God made Joshua a promise. He said, I have given the enemy into your hands, do not be afraid of them. After an all-night march, Joshua took the enemy by surprise. Wait a minute! After an all-night march, he still had some strategy in him and fight! Many people lose their strategy, let alone fight and start complaining after a 5-minute walk. You cannot give the bare minimum and still expect the best from God. It doesn't work like that, not with our God.

After Joshua put in his best effort, God showed up and did what Joshua could not do. If you are not putting in your best effort while depending on God to do what you cannot do, you are daydreaming, pal!

God hurled large hail stones and killed more of the enemy than Joshua and his army combined. This was only after Joshua had put in his best. God will do for you what you cannot do for yourself after you have utilized what He already placed in you to the best of your ability. Some of the prayers we offer up to God were answered the day we were born. Let me explain that.

I heard a story of a certain young man who for a long time prayed for a job. One day an opportunity was available at a United Nations office and he applied to be considered. He was shortlisted among the successful applicants and invited to attend an interview. One of the nights before the interview, he had a dream in which God told him, you got this son, I have given you this job!

On the day of the interview, this young man was very much assured that God had already given him the job slept in on the morning of the interview and ended up arriving late at the interview venue. He was still confident he had the job because God said, I have given it to you. As we all know, you can never create a first impression the second time. He did not get the job. Now many people will say, maybe God did not give him the job? God did! In fact, God did His part. It was this young man's responsibility to wake up early on the day of the interview, make sure his clothes were organized and appropriate for the interview. It was his job to show up on time because, you see, God will only do for us what He knows we cannot do for ourselves. Getting up early to be at an interview in good time, that is on you. Many people lose God opportunities because of laziness. Here is another Bible story to further illustrate our part.

> The night before Herod was to bring him to trial, Peter was sleeping between two soldiers, bound with two chains, and sentries stood guard at the entrance. Suddenly an angel of the Lord appeared and a light shone in the cell. He struck Peter on the side and woke him up. "Quick, get up!" he said, and the chains fell off Peter's wrists. Then the angel said to him, "Put on your clothes and sandals." And Peter did so. "Wrap your cloak around you and follow me," the angel told him. Peter followed him out of the prison, but he had no idea that what the angel was doing was really happening; he thought he was seeing a vision. They passed the first and second guards and came to the iron gate leading to the city. It opened for them by itself, and they went through it. When they had walked the length of one street, suddenly the angel left him.

> **(Acts 12:6-10)**

I like this story because the Angel could have carried Peter from the jail house and placed him somewhere safe. But the Angel woke Peter up, broke the chains, then asked Peter to put on his clothes and sandals, wrap his cloak around him, then follow the Angel. The Angel helped Peter escape the jail house. Many people expect that God will dress them, brush their teeth, iron their clothes, get them to their destination on time, fix their bed. God is not your mother!

God is a good, good Father, but He expects His sons and daughters to do their part and not be lazy.

A lazy life is an empty life, but "early to rise" gets the job done.

(Proverbs 12:27 MSG)

Go to the ant, you sluggard; consider its ways and be wise! It has no commander, no overseer or ruler, yet it stores its provisions in summer and gathers its food at harvest. How long will you lie there, you sluggard? When will you get up from your sleep? A little sleep, a little slumber, a little folding of the hands to rest—and poverty will come on you like a thief and scarcity like an armed man.

(Proverbs 6:6-11)

When we planted Musaale Church, I used to commute from the city of Kampala every weekend to put on the church celebrations. I did this for the first seven months of the church plant. Then it started to dawn on me that this was not going to work long term unless I really worked it. I decided to leave my business and move to the most happening town, a.k.a

Mbale, in order to fulfill the great commission of making disciples. You see, you cannot disciple people from a distance. You can inspire and influence people from a distance on social media, but you cannot disciple them. Discipleship is not a study course either, it is a lifestyle and you cannot disciple people who do not know your lifestyle. This is why I knew I had to move. I needed to invest my life in the lives of the people who came to the church and it would be unrealistic for me to place certain expectations on them that I had not demonstrated. Many leaders get frustrated because they have high expectations of their team, but forget that without demonstration of expectation, desired results cannot be realized.

I needed to be in the lives of the people eight days a week for emphasis's sake, if I was going to see meaningful growth and transformation. Discipleship is not projecting your perfect self either. It is being who you are before people. With your strengths, talents, weaknesses, insecurities, fears, doubts on full display. Discipleship is clever vulnerability.

I later discovered that you have to be careful what fears and doubts and feelings and weaknesses you share when discipling people, because people will misunderstand you, and you will lose the whole point of discipleship because they will no longer view you as a moral authority in that area. Jesus was simple enough to be accessible and approachable, yet powerful enough to heal and meet the needs of His followers. A lot of the things I'm sharing in this book are things I have been through that have shaped me to become the man I am today. It does not mean I'm still that man. I'm not perfect, I'm a work in progress, but I have overcome much and paid the price much. You have to pay your price too. Many people think you become like Jesus miraculously by laying on of hands. It's not true. It is a long process.

People will place you on a pedestal and it is your responsibility to correct that, but to be clever about it too. How you share your weaknesses, your doubts and your fears matters. Who you share with matters too. You have to gauge the growth levels of the people working the dream with you. We have to lead with humility, but we must be firm and strong and create a Kingdom environment of honor. I shared in the previous verse about confronting people. Discipleship is confronting that which God exposes, which is limiting people on your team and so limiting the team overall, so that they can grow and become what God wants them to be and the team can be effective.

Ultimately, people should see your commitment to God as an individual and want the same. They should see your excellent work ethic and want the same. Some will see and still not get it. They are a hard nut to crack.

Eventually, with some persuasion, some pressure and heat, people break and are awakened. God knows how to bring on that pressure and heat perfectly. You just keep being consistent and faithful as a leader and leave the results up to God. You can control your own performance, but not the performance of others.

You also have to be very patient with people. Some of the things you demonstrate as a dreamer/leader, you learned over a long period of time. Don't expect people to get it in a week, a few weeks or even a few months. It will take years for many people to really get what you are really on about or get to know who you really are.

Bearing fruit!

A lot of what I do now I learned over many years. I shared earlier that I have so far been to 5 continents of the world and many countries and cities. I have also visited countless churches of all denominations and styles. I have led some really successful fundraising and mission tours. These missions have given me an accumulated experience that allows me to perform at a certain level, with a certain work ethic and worldview that is quite frankly rare in all parts of the world. I hold myself to certain expectations that it would be unfair for me to expect that exact same performance from someone who has not had similar experiences. With time and observation, though, I will expect that they get at least a bit, if not a fair bit of it. God will never hold you accountable for things He has not revealed to you and taught you yet. God comes looking for fruit because He made an investment, and we should expect fruit from our teams so that we are not wasting our efforts. God doesn't like waste. You see this by how He treats the one talented man who refused to invest and multiply his talent. He was not willing to pay the price involved with making dreams happen. God sends him to the outer darkness where there is gnashing of teeth.

"Therefore, I tell you that the kingdom of God will be taken away from you and given to a people who will produce its fruit.

(Matthew 21:43)

When God makes an investment, He comes looking for fruit. When God places dreams in our hearts, He prepares us to make the dream work. Joseph was prepared through the incredible adversity he faced. I mean daddy's favorite boy thrown in a ditch, then sold as a slave, then mopping floors, then falsely accused of rape and imprisoned for it. Could it get any worse? Joseph did not give up on God and his dreams and neither should you or I.

Basing on my own experience, when you are being prepared, it rarely looks like preparation. It looks more like punishment for sin, sometimes like betrayal and malice. You could end up beating yourself up, thinking you did something wrong to deserve it to the point you cannot receive what God offers you. It is easy to disqualify yourself from what God qualifies you for. Sometimes, I'm so hard on myself that I think it even amazes the devil. That is why God asks us to let go of past mistakes and hurts, to forgive. Forgive others and forgive ourselves. Joseph, the dreamer, only saw suffering for a while and probably asked God why. The Bible says Joseph still maintained an excellent spirit. Holding on to un-forgiveness and anger and bitterness will hinder us big time. Part of paying the price, carrying our cross, is learning to forgive, to let go of a bitter spirit. When Joseph finally meets his brothers, later on, we see why he was made prime minister of Egypt. He did not hold bitterness toward his brothers. He was able to receive because he had let go. Joseph was a free man. You have to learn to rise above the tide of adversity in order to live the dream.

His brothers then came and threw themselves down before him. "We are your slaves," they said. But

Joseph said to them, "Don't be afraid. Am I in the place of God? You intended to harm me, but God intended it for good to accomplish what is now being done, the saving of many lives. So then, don't be afraid. I will provide for you and your children." And he reassured them and spoke kindly to them.

(Genesis 50:18-21)

Has God been preparing you for a task, but you do not know it? Is He asking you to do something and you are making excuses? If you look back over your life, take a real good look at all your past experiences. The painful experiences, the losses, the relationship breakups that left you deeply heartbroken, you will see God has been preparing you for what He is asking of you now. In equal measure, holding on to the guilt of deliberate mistakes will hinder us big time. Guilt will make you disqualify yourself from what God has qualified you for. I don't know how many times God has asked me to go after something He wanted to give me, but I felt inadequate for it. Instead of receiving what God was offering, I went on a repenting, fasting and praying spree trying to be pious, and this over things I had overcome a long time ago. The Bible calls that being sin-conscious. God must laugh at some of our religious efforts to demonstrate devotion to Him when we should just be receiving His grace and kindness with gratefulness.

See to it that no one fails to obtain the grace of God; that no root of bitterness springs up and causes trouble, and through it, many become defiled.

(Hebrews 12:15)

When God gives you something, He already knows you. In fact, God knows us better than we know ourselves. It is of absolute importance to forgive yourself or else you will disqualify yourself from what God has qualified you for. God will not force anything on you. He will just take you around the mountain again in the hope that you get it. God looks at our not receiving as looking down on His offer of grace. What we do not value, we tend to lose. Kind of like Esau did not value his birthright and exchanged it for a bowl of lentils in what was the worst recorded business deal ever in the history of mankind.

"Guilt will make you disqualify yourself from what God has qualified you for."

David was anointed king over Israel but spent years running away from Saul. He was being prepared to live the dream. David wandered in the wilderness, even pretending to have lost his mind at one point so he could save his life. Okay, this guy had been anointed king of Israel, he had killed Goliath and saved the nation, and is now playing insane to save his life, the kingship looks so far from him, but no, he will be king as God said. Find the story in 1 Samuel 21.

God doesn't waste any experience, but many of the experiences, the delays will not make sense. God will never expect you to perform at a level He has not already prepared you to perform. David had to carry the cross of the wilderness before he could assume the comforts of the palace as King of Israel.

When I was maybe ten years old, I got to learn of some distant relatives immigrating to the United Kingdom. I said to myself. I would never fully immigrate and permanently live in another country. I said if I did go to other countries outside Uganda, there would have to be a higher purpose for me, and I would still always return to Uganda. 13 years later, I started traveling the world to raise awareness and support for the AIDS orphans of Uganda. I spent between 6 to 10 months on tours and would return to Uganda at the end of every tour. I was traveling on purpose, raising awareness and support, plus sharing the good news of the hope that is found in Jesus Christ. I was also being prepared for the life God always had in mind for me to live, which I'm living now.

Every experience God gives you is meant to lead you to the next thing. God never wastes His investments. On my first trip around the world, I had never worked so hard. I was exhausted. I wanted to give up. I'm a driven person and like to perform, to get things done. Part of the motivation growing up was always to prove myself. It gave me a sense of the importance of getting a job done well.

I performed for approval and acceptance, but this was a tough gig. I wanted to quit.

We sometimes slept on church floors, and in some instances, you would find yourself dancing over the very space you would be laying your head the same night. When I pondered quitting, I also remembered where I came from and how being in the center of London, England was a miracle. I snapped out of it and kept on going. Many people give up on things because they have not rationally looked at the full story. Trusting God does not take away difficulty or rationality, but it should make us stronger and wiser. As someone one said,

"Life doesn't get easier. You get stronger."

God taught me endurance, perseverance of character through the rigorous schedule I had to adapt to. I started to build some stability and strength of character and some "sticktivitis" (sticking with things and seeing them through), that I did not have in me. Up to this point, giving up what I found difficult and painful was part of my way of life because I did not have a personal value system. When things were uncomfortable, escapism was the way. You have to be careful with people who have nothing to lose. I was one like that for a long time until this started to happen. God was building character in me that I needed for today, and today He is building character in me that I need for tomorrow.

When you look back over your life, you will see that God was preparing you for the life He wanted you to live. He was calling you, prompting you, wanting to win you to Himself. Some people are a hard nut to crack. They don't get it. The good thing about God is He is patient. He will give you time, create the right circumstances to corner you and help you change so you can fulfill the purposes He created you for. Many people who do not fulfill their purpose in God persist in their stubbornness and God won't force His will and divine methods on anyone.

"The servant who knows the master's will and does not get ready or does not do what the master wants will be beaten with many blows. But the one who does not know and does things deserving

punishment will be beaten with few blows. From everyone who has been given much, much will be demanded; and from the one who has been entrusted with much, much more will be asked.

(Luke 12:47-48)

Every experience God gives you, He wants to use in you for others. Every blessing God gives, He wants you to be a conduit He can work through to pass on to others. The knowledge and revelations you get from God about God He wants you to turn around and share. It is God's multiplication principle. That is why an avocado tree bears fruit with seed and that seed becomes another avocado tree. When Jesus was hungry and looked for figs on a fig tree and did not find any, he cursed it dry. Why? In my opinion, it was because that which is not fulfilling its purpose is taking up valuable space. Mel Gibson playing William Wallace in the movie Braveheart says,

"All men die; few men ever really live."
_ _ Braveheart (The Movie)

Personal devotion!

You must be sure to invest in yourself so that you can continually have something to offer. Invest in personal study and devotion so that your public ministry display is an overflow of your private life. When God started leading me to plant the church, I knew that I needed to increase my prayer time and my Bible reading. I needed to create a constant fellowship with God so that I would have something from Him to offer those I lead. I started a personal compulsory 5:30 AM prayer. This is my date time with God. I read a couple of chapters in the Bible and pray. I do this religiously whenever 5:30 AM comes, wherever I may be at the time. I have done this on an Airbus A380 bound for Brisbane, Australia, and I have done it time and again on an Airbus A380 bound for Los Angeles, California and Houston, Texas. Sometimes I do not say much. I just honor the time I have set to spend with God in the morning. If you do not make an effort to grow and seek God more as a leader, you risk doing your own thing and what a waste that is. There is a high risk of burnout with that too. I heard Casey Treat say that his primary responsibility as a pastor is not to preach or lead the church. His primary responsibility is to keep God first in his life. Everything else works out as he makes his relationship with God the priority of his life. I could not agree more. God calls us to Himself first, then to the ministry. Like the Macedonia church, *They gave themselves first to God and then to the ministry.*

Many people think when God calls you, He will also automatically impart the strength and anointing you need for the work, so you are always on a full tank coursing through ministry. It's not necessarily true. God will visit you, fill you, but you have to make yourself available, to show God you want to be effective for Him, to invest in yourself to learn and grow. You must hunger for God and show Him you are serious about what He has called you to. You must show God ownership. God said to me once when I was asking questions during my financial struggles. He said, I will allow you to experience financial struggle and other struggles, I will withhold some comforts and conveniences from you so that you can do the work not just because I said so, and because I blessed you, but because you know that you have a stake in it, you have ownership of it. I take issue with people who think they are doing God a favor when they get involved in serving in ministry. We do not do God a favor. He does us a favor by involving us and then turning around and rewarding us for it with a well done good and faithful servant.

Everything God teaches us, He wants us to pass on to others. This is how disciples are grown. Again, you cannot give what you do not have, and God does not expect you to give what you don't have. You must pay the price.

I have seen people in leadership trying to act like they know certain things that they actually don't because they want to paint the image to their followers that they know everything. As a dreamer/leader, you have to remember you are not the star of your own dream; Christ Jesus is. He is the dream giver and the dream maker. Christ is the ultimate teacher, the one who knows everything. I am at my best when I can point my team to the One who knows all things, so we are all receiving from Him. The reason we have a team is because we cannot do everything and so cannot know everything. When I started to get comfortable with not knowing some things, I started to become more effective and more secure as a leader. The things I know, the things that pertain to the overall vision of the church, I share with my whole heart. I put all of my energy in those because I know that if I'm not a good steward of the things God has given me and taught me, I will be beaten with many blows, as brother

Luke says in Luke 12. We must pay the price of the dream God gives us, embracing the pain and discomfort that comes along in all the shapes and forms it comes because everything adds up to accomplishing God's big picture for our lives.

Chapter 11

Running Your Race

I t is not how you start out in life that matters, it is how you finish that counts. You are not in charge of how you start, but you are in charge of how you continue on in life to the finish line. Where you are born is not an issue or limitation with what God can do with you. It can be an issue with people and how they relate to you, but not with God. God knew you. He saw you like Hagar when she says, "You are the God who sees me" in Genesis 16:13. God set a plan in motion for our lives the moment we were conceived. He planned our geography so that wherever we are, we would call on the name of the one who saves all mankind. In order to walk in God's purpose in our lives, we must get on His path for us and learn to stay the path he has designed for us to walk. Not drifting to the left or right, but staying in the center of His will for us.

*Do you not know that in a race, everyone runs, but
only one gets the prize? So run to win!*

(1 Corinthians 9:24)

The race we run to fulfill the purpose God placed us on planet earth for is cut out specifically for us and no one else can run it. There is no competition on the track God has designed for you and I to run. This is not a rat race. It is destiny. If there is competition at all, then it is us competing with who we were yesterday so that we outrun who we were yesterday and embrace who we are meant to be today and tomorrow. If you do not run your race, yesterday will catch up and run over you and keep you stagnated and unable to fulfill your purpose.

*"I knew you before I formed you in your mother's
womb.
Before you were born, I set you apart
and appointed you as my prophet to the nations."*

(Jeremiah 1:5)

No one ever chooses what family to be born into. "I'll be born to the rich guy that makes the Whitehouse God, okay! Or the guy they call the richest man on planet earth, those are my choices, God, okay!" Said no one ever!

No one chooses their country, their clan if they have one, their village, their nationality, their tribe, we all came here at the will of someone else, and God knew we were coming and had a plan in motion for us. There are many people in the church around the globe asking to know their purpose in life. The only way to discover it is by getting on the path God has for you and staying the course in season and out of season. How do I get on that path, you might ask?

First, you did this by getting into a relationship with God through His only begotten Son, Jesus Christ. I shared a prayer in the introduction of this book which was meant to be a guide to starting a relationship with God through His Son Jesus Christ. If you did not say that prayer then and mean it, I would like to give you another opportunity to say it now so you can take the first step towards the path God has for you. If you have been saved a zillion years, say it anyway. I have everyone say this prayer at my church every time I preach and it has never hurt anyone.

> **Lord Jesus, I am a sinner. I have failed you. I have lived for myself and not for your glory. Forgive me of my sin, come into my heart, be my Lord and my Savior. Help me to live for you from this day forth. I receive you now with a thankful heart. In Jesus' most beautiful name, Amen!**

In track and field competitions, all contestants are assigned a specific track they must adhere to in the race or risk disqualification. Getting on the path God has for you is not rocket science. It's simply an acknowledgment of your need to be saved and to be included in God's divine plan for humanity. Life really and truly begins when we say yes to Jesus! If you just said the prayer to receive Jesus and mean it, you have started the most beautiful journey of your life. Please find a life-giving church near you and join the fellowship of believers, God's family on planet earth. Let them know you have decided to follow Jesus and you want to be part of God's great big family. If you have been saved a zillion years, let us carry on running this race as to win it.

I must warn you and many who have been saved a while will say this, that giving your heart to Jesus is exciting and you are going to feel goosebumps along with all kinds of good feelings, but you will also start to recognize all the bad, sinful stuff about you and will feel really horrible even hopeless against them. It's not like these things were not in your life before, they were there, but you were complicit to them in your life without Christ. We all are complicit to sin before Christ comes into our lives. A life outside of Christ is a life that is united as one with sinful flesh. But a life that has surrendered to Christ will start to be convicted of sin unto righteousness. It is like living in a dark cave and then one day, a bright light shines through it. You will notice things you did not see before the light came on. This is what happens or should happen throughout our Christian lives following Jesus and being transformed into His likeness. It doesn't matter how long you have been saved, if the Spirit of God is not highlighting attitudes and mentalities He wants you to change, then you have settled short. We are daily being transformed. The things the Holy Spirit exposes were there, but the darkness concealed them. Kind of like the stars, but in reverse. The stars are always there in the sky, but it is the darkness of night that reveals them. The darker it gets, the clearer the stars. This is why you need to join a life-giving church and get proper guidance on your journey so you can learn and grow and run your race.

Disillusionment

When I first gave my heart to Jesus, I had a lot of assumptions about the church. I knew in my heart that following Jesus meant I would have to let go of certain sinful practices in my life. I knew that lying was wrong, stealing was wrong, cheating was wrong, fornication was wrong. No one told me all these things when I got saved. I just knew that they were wrong and had to go. This made me make assumptions about those I found in the church and had been saved for many years. The first time I witnessed someone who I knew had been saved and in the church for a long time, one I looked at as a potential someone to learn from about my new found faith, when I heard that they cheated someone of money or have been involved in fornication, I was shocked and disappointed, I could not believe it. I thought people who got saved automatically stopped these things. But the disappointment did not stop there. I started to notice some people would not keep their word. They would borrow money and not payback. They would gossip and backstab each other. You see, I thought that becoming a Christian would automatically change someone's character, but I have learned over the years, character grows on purpose. Hearts change by will, not automatically.

When I looked at my own life, I realized the things I wanted to go were not leaving without a fight. I was struggling with sexual sin. I was a people pleaser, so lying had a hold on me, I thought up some horribly bad ideas, plus I ended up intentionally cheating someone of their money, giving them less than I should have in a business transaction.

I was a cheater too. The disillusionment was not just about the people I saw who had been in the church for a long time. It was in me too. I thought these things would fall off of me the day I said yes to Jesus, but alas, no! I was a hypocrite too! What was I going to do? I was going to keep running the race because transformation happens as you stay in the race. Staying in the race is continually working out your salvation as the Spirit of God works in you to produce the fruit of the Kingdom.

There's another form of disillusionment I experienced after I gave my heart to Jesus. I had felt unconditional warmth and love and acceptance like I had never felt before on that Easter Sunday. I thought to myself, and this is in regards to everyone else, "You would be a fool not to want this." But when I went to college to study for my diploma in business, otherwise called an associate's degree in business at the Uganda College of Commerce, and started to share my faith, students laughed at me for sharing my faith. In fact, they did more; they scoffed at me, ridiculed me, said I was a bluff. I had only shared with them the good news of the unconditional love of God that I had experienced. How could anyone ridicule something as beautiful as that, I thought. Then again, how could I have been so naive to think that they would get it? That is when it started to dawn on me that Christianity is not only running a race, but it is a spiritual war. We are spirit beings residing in a physical body. Our spirit is either aligned to God and His Kingdom or to this world and its ways.

Embracing the risen Christ is declaring war on the powers of darkness and the enemy will fight 24/7 to try and keep you operating under the spirit of this world in order to undermine your Christian testimony. He will try to water down your experience until the feelings you experienced when you made the confession to give your heart to Jesus means nothing to you. The devil means business. We wage war by staying in the race, running the track assigned to us, continually being transformed by Jesus. Giving your heart to Jesus is declaring war on the spirit of this world! It is declaring to this world," I have decided to follow Jesus!" The good news is, it's not our war. In fact, it is an already won war. Christ Jesus won the war when He went to the cross, was buried, descended into darkness and took the keys from the devil in a display of superiority, making the enemy kneel down in surrender in his own house, and then rose from the dead on the third day. Instead of trying so hard to be victorious, we must surrender to the one who overcame so that His victory over sin and the world becomes ours too. The Christian life is the exchanged life. We are not alone in our race. God has made it such that we run on the fuel of the Holy Spirit, who is our strength. On your own, you cannot really be a Christian. We do not have it in our flesh to be Jesus' followers. No matter how much good you do, it will not keep the devil from trying to mess up your life. But the life-giving presence of Jesus, the Holy Spirit, empowers us to overcome this world, to stay on track and keep running the race to a victorious finish.

> *I have been crucified with Christ and I no longer live, but Christ lives in me. The life I now live in the body, I live by faith in the Son of God, who loved me and gave himself for me.*

I do not set aside the grace of God, for if righteousness could be gained through the law, Christ died for nothing!"

(Galatians 2:20-21)

The day we give our hearts to Jesus, we die to this world and become alive to the Kingdom of Heaven. However, this is not an instant death. We die daily as we make an effort to stay the course. After my disillusionment with folks who had been in church for years and then my own disillusionment as a hypocrite, I did not give up, but made an effort to learn more. I'm still on that journey, learning and growing. You have read about some of my struggles in earlier chapters. I have seen some people give up making an effort to grow and have embraced a shallow Christianity because of what they discovered from the people they found already in the faith. Don't copy what you find. Write your own story. Christianity is not copy and paste. It is personal. You will make mistakes, but keep making an effort to become the person God created you to be.

I later on in my walk started to discover some people had just settled for the shallow end of the faith and stayed there because they couldn't bother making an effort to confront the uncomfortable. They were lazy Christians. They never ventured into the deep end because the deep end was not safe. It is uncomfortable and inconvenient. It will expose you, shake you and reveal your weaknesses for the world to see. The deep end will embarrass you, break you, humiliate you, but it will also refine you as it shakes off the things that you held onto that do not please God. You will not fulfill your calling in Christ by staying in the shallow end of fear and comfort.

The week after I got saved, I started reading the Bible and loved every bit of it I read. Reading the Bible revealed me and rebuked me in a way I had always wanted to be rebuked. The kind of rebuke that means you well. For a long time, I longed for something real and authentic because I could see myself as a fake, a pretender. I grew up wanting to be corrected when I made mistakes. I needed guidance but never got it. Like I said in the beginning, I grew up by accident. Reading proverbs was refreshing! Nothing knocks you on the head like the book of Proverbs. I chewed on it like good food that first week after I got saved and continued. I heard from a couple I stayed with in a town in Australia that reads the book of Proverbs every month. They read a chapter a day because it keeps them aligned with the truth. I say more power to that! Proverbs showed me just how much foolishness I had walked in all my life up to that point and had called it being sharp. Some of the things an upside world calls amazing and upright are simply evil and self-destructive.

Better to be an ordinary person with a servant than to be self-important but have no food.

(Proverbs 12:9)

When I read this scripture, I laughed till I cried because I could see myself in it. Like I mentioned earlier, I was not proud of my family because of my earthly father's alcoholism. I wanted to be part of another family and often pretended to be. I pretended to be someone else, but went home and had no food, lol!

Oh, the freedom I have found in finally embracing who I was and where I came from, and who I am daily becoming in Christ. It doesn't all happen at once. It's been a long journey folks. God wants to give you a story to tell of how He rescued you and helped you so that others may be encouraged to run their own race and not give up. God said to me several years ago,

> **"There are people counting on you. People you have not even met yet, they are counting on you, son."**

I want to keep running my race with perseverance and hope so that I can help as many people as I am meant to in this life, so I can be a light in the world for the glory of our great and awesome God.

Christianity is war!

If you are going to stay the course and become the man/woman God wants you to be, you must brace yourself for it. You must decide and resolve in your heart that you will not be dissuaded or persuaded, you are following Jesus and there is no turning back. You must decide that you are not living for anyone else, but for Jesus. Let the world say what they say, let the world throw at you what it throws, you have decided and you are not looking back. God is waiting for you to make that decision because He will not make it for you.

The devil is relentless, never gives up. He knows where you are coming from. He knows what tripped you, what you struggled with in the past. The devil wants to hold you to your history before coming to Christ so that you give up on your destiny in Christ. He wants to freeze you in your tracks, so you stop running and simply give up, saying this does not make any sense or it doesn't work. **Christianity is war!**

When I gave my heart to Jesus, I knew that I was called to full-time ministry right away. My commitment was solid. You wouldn't convince me otherwise. But there was still deliberate compromise with things like pornography and masturbation. I was a liar. The flesh had a hold on me. What made my struggles even worse was I had strong convictions and so came off to people as a man of faith. I projected my ideal self to people. Bishop T.D Jakes says in one of his sermons, *"Some folks project their ideal self to people, then they go home and pray about their real self."*

I was one of those folks for a long time. Deep inside, I knew I was a fake, I was deliberately compromising, I was also a liar, it was pathetic, I needed help and I knew it! I confessed my struggles to God, asking that between me and Him, He would set me free without embarrassing me. Ever felt like that? At times, I won a victory and was free for a little while, but would relapse after a week or a month. If I stood firm for over a month or so, I felt upright. Freedom from sin is not a battle God wants you to fight on your own, because you will lose every time if you do. Plus, keeping score of how long you have stayed free from the sins you are embarrassed about does not take them away. Acknowledging your shortcomings, giving them to Jesus and submitting in surrender to His strength is what gives us ultimate victory.

Transparency!

Therefore confess your sins to each other and pray for each other so that you may be healed. The prayer of a righteous person is powerful and effective.

(James 5:16)

Something of the divine happens in our lives when we act human because, we actually are human. When we become vulnerable and confess our failures, we start to have victory over things that have held us back for years. The things you hold on to and don't talk about will keep having a hold on you. The day you start to confide in someone else and be open about your struggles is the day your healing and freedom will start to flow like a river. It's like God has made it that when people can see our humanness, when we are vulnerable, then He will release more of His power in our lives.

God resists the proud, but gives grace to the humble.

(James 4:8).

The beauty of humanity is not in our perfection, but in our brokenness and sincere dependence on the divine presence and power of almighty God. When I stopped being ashamed of my sin and openly spoke about my struggles, I started to experience freedom. One of the enemy's lies to us is, "You are in this alone. You are a pervert and it is only you dealing with this. You are alone. You are embarrassing." When I started to be honest about my own struggles, I discovered other people became comfortable sharing their own struggles with me. They were human, too, after all. We were all human and God loved us enough to die for us. Oh, the freedom you will experience when you start to go down the path of being open with your weaknesses and sin. That doesn't mean you start declaring your struggles openly to everyone. You have to identify people you can confide in. People of character, people you see, are making an effort to be all that God wants them to be. If you confide in someone who is not making an effort, you might just be encouraged to continue in your sin. Be honest with a pastor or leader in the church you know is living upright and is full of the spirit. Do whatever you can to be free. It takes humbling ourselves. I would rather humble myself, than wait for God to humiliate me. Whatever is exposed to the light loses its power. Whatever is not exposed stays to wreak havoc in the dark places of our lives.

But everything exposed by the light becomes visible—
and everything that is illuminated becomes a light.

(Ephesians 5:13)

God is counting on you to put your best foot forward, to do everything in your ability to live a life that honors Him as you run your race. The more I have become honest about my struggles, the more I found freedom. There is life in light, but death in darkness.

Running away

When I started to critically look at areas and things in my life that caused me to stumble or to have desires that led me down the cycle of sin and shame, I started to make a deliberate effort to avoid those places. In fact, I started to flee from anything suggestive and not give it a second look. That magazine, that internet pop up, that junk email. When God sees that you are doing what you can, He will supply the strength you did not have before to help you on the journey. We empower in our lives what we open ourselves to. If we open ourselves to God, we invite His strength to overcome the world.

I read John Eldredge's book, *Wild at Heart,* and he says pornography is not about hormones, but about fear and cowardice. You are afraid of the commitment that comes with getting involved with a real person. You are afraid a real person will see your weaknesses and vulnerable points, so you would rather relate with an image of someone who won't present any challenge to you but make themselves freely available to you and give you total control of the experience. Make sense? It did to me.

When I read that portion in his book, I looked at my own life and I had been a chicken for a long time. Growing up afraid to embrace my true family identity made me afraid of a lot of other things in life, including being vulnerable. Having a false sense of control was more appealing to me than being vulnerable. One day God said to me, "You control nothing." Yes, just like that! Isn't that just the truth of humanity? We control nothing. God controls everything! He's got the whole world in His hands! Did you know that controlling people are just cowards and being in control is a cover-up? I have never met a controlling person who had nothing to hide. Control is some form of compensation, but Jesus wants to be our full and complete compensation, so we do not have to feel like we have to be in control to feel valuable. We are valuable in Christ because He completes us, covering for every deficiency in our frail, broken, sinful human frames.

If you met me today, you might think that I fell down from Heaven, already perfected and ready to run this race called life hahahaha.

As you can see from reading on my life's journey, you do not become a strong mature Christian in a day, a week, a month, a year. It takes a lifetime of running away from the past and running into the future God has for you. You will overcome things as you stay running your track. When you stop running, you stop overcoming. The things of the past will come wanting to catch up. There is no neutral place in the Kingdom. The future is always calling us to keep reaching. As you keep reaching, you will start to look down on things that had you in their grasp. As you keep running, you grow and start to see your value as a child of God. You see royalty. Spiritual transformation is God giving us a new perspective on the things that held us captive. Kind of like when I was a kid, I was sometimes convinced there was a lion in my bedroom and it was going to eat me. The shadow of that shirt on a hanger looked very much like a leopard, but when I grew up, I know it's just a shirt. I know this is not so deep, but you get my point.

In God's eyes, all things are Holy and when we get God's perspective on life and things, everything becomes beautiful because we see it as we should, not through eyes of sin and shame. The pornography industry thrives on showing nakedness and sex, but God created the human body fearfully and wonderfully, male and female, each to fulfill their purpose in a covenant love relationship. Sex is not evil. It is holy. God invented it, not Hollywood. Everything God made is holy and can be used to fulfill its true purpose or can be abused and misused. Abuse and misuse always comes with consequences and much of the mess in the world is because of abuse and misuse of the beautiful things and the life God has entrusted humanity with. Spiritual transformation is starting to see life and things from God's point of view. It is a lifelong commitment.

Therefore let him who thinks he stands to take heed lest he fall.

(1 Corinthians 10:12)

Chapter 12

Just Keep Running!

I have often asked myself questions like; When will I stop struggling? When will I just start coursing effortlessly through life? Will there ever be a time when I stop dealing with sin? When will my judgment on life and things and people be perfectly upright? It is easy as pastors to try and create a facade of perfection in order to earn the confidence of our followers, but God is okay with you just being you. What people think is of no consequence to what God does with us. The right people will recognize what God has placed inside of you and how that helps connect them to you. The truth is, as long as we are in this human form and have not upgraded to eternity, we will always have to contend with sin and our fallenness. It is an ever-present reminder that, left on our own, we humans will self-destruct. But what is even more ever-present is the cross. The finished work on the cross answered all the questions to our human struggles. The only way to keep going is, to be honest, vulnerable and open to the Spirit of God who ministers life to us.

Therefore we also, since we are surrounded by so great a cloud of witnesses, let us lay aside every weight, and the sin which so easily ensnares us, and let us run with endurance the race that is set before us, looking unto Jesus, the author and finisher of our faith, who for the joy that was set before Him endured the cross, despising the shame, and has sat down at the right hand of the throne of God. For consider Him who endured such hostility from sinners against Himself, lest you become weary and discouraged in your souls.

(Hebrews 12:1-3)

I mentioned that when my earthly father died, I did not want him to go even though I had spent my life embarrassed about him and wishing I was an orphan. My earthly father had received Jesus and we had started a healthy relationship where he would call me and we would pray on the phone. Jesus gave me the earthly father I had always wanted. He redeemed decades of shame in a matter of months. Getting real with my dad, as I mentioned earlier, confessing my shame and embarrassment towards him, plus asking for forgiveness, brought light between us and disarmed the powers of darkness. It allowed God to come in and bring healing between us. Remember James 5:16? "Confess your sins one to another so that you may be healed." God healed my relationship with my dad and helped me embrace my true earthly identity without shame or embarrassment when I allowed the truth to come between my dad and I. This has been the blueprint of all my relationships. Honesty is the greatest foundation for meaningful connections in life. I know my earthly father is in Heaven with my Heavenly Father now, but I'm grateful the memories between us are healed and beautiful. God turns ugly stories into beautiful ones if we let Him.

Honesty will help you find freedom. Denial will keep you in bondage and will escalate your struggles even more. Some people think that denying or hiding their struggles helps them overcome, but what you hide under the carpet stays where you hid it until you come back and take out the carpet. Time does not heal anything either. If you have beef with someone else because they offended you deeply, acknowledge it, talk about it and with the intention to address it, so it does not have power over you. Some people talk about who offended them only to show that they are the good guys. They have no intention to address the issue and be free, just to capitalize on the offense. The devil likes this because he knows he can control such people and keep them ineffective in serving their purpose. He can slow them down, even bring them to a complete halt.

Unwillingness to confront past shame and embarrassment no matter what it is because you think it is too much to deal with will cripple your ability to run your race. It is in acknowledging and dealing with our own brokenness that we learn to relate to other people's brokenness. It is in addressing our own weakness and error that we can help others deal with their own weakness and errors. Healed people heal people, just like hurt people hurt people. God's power is released to us and for us when we make the decision to confront. Most difficult people who are hard to get along with are going through the crisis of unresolved issues. They just don't know it. They think everyone else is the problem but themselves.

Accepting your history will give you God's picture of you and everything from God's point of view is beautiful.

Denying your history because of its shame only cripples the potential of the future and can make you a difficult person to deal with or get along with. The past is supposed to be used as a step to the future. What the enemy intended for evil being turned into good as God's deliverance work in your life encourages others to run their race. In the Bible, we read of people who overcame in their generation. Joseph, Joshua, Paul, Peter, lives that were turned around and used greatly by God. Our lives are living epistles for others to see and be inspired to run their own race as to finish it. So keep running, keep confronting because you never know who is watching.

When I started to accept my family background along with the embarrassment and shame involved, the shame and embarrassment started to lose its power over me. It is wonderful to embrace your sonship in Christ. But if you reject your earthly family, you are rejecting your Nazareth. You are forfeiting your story and your strength. This is why Peter and John, when they healed the man at the gate called beautiful, used the identity of the only name that saves and heals and delivers.

Then Peter said, "Silver and gold I do not have, but what I do have I give you: In the name of Jesus Christ of Nazareth, rise up and walk." And he took him by the right hand and lifted him up, and immediately his feet and ankle bones received strength. So he, leaping up, stood and walked and entered the temple with them — walking, leaping, and praising God. And all the people saw him walking and praising God. Then they knew that it was he who sat begging alms at the Beautiful Gate of the temple; and they were filled with wonder and amazement at what had happened to him.

(Acts 3:6-10)

Only Jesus Christ of Nazareth has the power to make crippled people walk. The Jesus of Portugal or Brazil has no power to save humanity. It is Jesus of Nazareth. Your destiny is tied to your identity and no one can be you. I'm only as effective as I should be as the man born in Mbale, the most happening place in Uganda, to the family I was born to. If you are going to truly find your lane and keep it, you will have to go all the way back to where the lies began. God loves to take us into our past before He takes us into our future. When God starts to bring your past up, don't rebuke the devil saying it's backwardness. I did that for a long time, seeing myself back in my childhood home in dreams. When God takes you back there, he is bringing to your attention things that you ignored about yourself. Things that hurt you, things that affected you, lies that you believed. God will take you back in order to bring you forward because your life not only matters now, but it mattered then. The past is connected to the future and revisiting it makes sense of the future.

Jesus of Nazareth spells identity. There are many people who have called themselves Jesus, but only this Jesus, the Christ of Nazareth, has the power to raise the lame off the ground and get them walking, to heal the sick, to deliver the oppressed, to set captives free, to comfort the afflicted, and to raise the dead. Only this Jesus of Nazareth can do that. God has a specific role for you to fulfill that no one else can fulfill. One that has your name on it, one that will change the world and bring Him glory. This is why we have to keep running and confronting the uncomfortable places even when it feels like it's too much to deal with because it is in becoming more of who God created us to be that we can fulfill God's purpose for us. You will not fulfill your purpose pretending to be someone else because dealing with your stuff is too much for you to handle. Steven Furtick says it well; *"God will not bless who you pretend to be."*

The only way my story can be a blessing to anyone who hears or reads it is that it is relatable. I always thought that the things that really impact people are the good sides of us, the wonderful things God does, the victories we experience, but people who are struggling cannot relate to your victories. When people see my struggles and my failures and my weaknesses, and my victories too because God has been good to me, they can relate. I really hope you can relate to a thing or two in my story as you keep running your own.

I have been walking with Jesus coming up to 22 years now, and you would think that because I have been involved in full-time ministry and God has used me around the world, that I'm all that and a bag of chips and get everything God says to me by now, but I don't. I still don't get what God is on about many times. I make mistakes. I misunderstand what He is saying or doing, I get frustrated, sometimes angry, then I question my commitment to Him. Am I for real? I often ask myself! Sometimes I think I'm some kind of fraud pretending to represent God. I have also realized, it doesn't matter how long you have walked with God, how many things you have overcome and how many victories you have had. The devil will never stop fighting you. The more you grow, the more sophisticated the devil gets too. I mentioned earlier that when we planted the church, I saw in a dream the devil setting up a war station similar to what you see in the movie Braveheart with sharp arrows. Then after years of prayer and persistence and the church growing, I saw him depart with his sharp arrows. The enemy attacks in stages and phases and that stage was over. We had prevailed. Like one preacher said, *"Another level, another devil."*

The devil advances his tactics as we grow and advance in our faith. He will never stop lying to you and lying about you. Deception is his number one weapon. As long as we keep our focus on Jesus and keep believing the truth, the devil will always lose. After all, the devil is the eternal loser, I always say. His destiny is set for eternal damnation. We have a glorious destiny in Heaven with Jesus. Just keep running. As St Teresa of Avila said, *"When the devil reminds you of your past, remind him of his future."*

Finding your path and staying on it takes determination and resolve. It will cost you everything. This is why Jesus said to everyone who wanted to follow him to count the cost before they committed. God has no time for games, for testing to see if it works. You are either all in or all out, no in-betweens. Finding and committing to your path is the best thing you could ever do. There is nothing in all the world as beautiful and as fulfilling as being in the center of God's will for you. You owe it to yourself to make every effort to get on that path, whatever it costs. You will find that being in the center of God's will for you is worth more than anything you give up on or walk away from. You cannot outdo God!

He who loves father or mother more than Me is not worthy of Me. And he who loves son or daughter more than Me is not worthy of Me. And he who does not take his cross and follow after Me is not worthy of Me. He who finds his life will lose it, and he who loses his life for My sake will find it.

(Matthew 10:37-39)

When I was really young, I always thought I would do things to help people, to change lives. That's what I did for seven years, raising awareness and support for the AIDS orphans of Africa. In the last ten years since I quit my cool job at Watoto, together with support from friends, we have built a primary school and are in the process of building a high school in my mother's ancestral village to provide a decent school environment and quality education. We have built a community center to help women learn a trade they can use to create an income for themselves. Through my business, I've been able to sponsor a number of kids to get an education. Musaale Church is growing at our two campuses, and I am on a mission with God to explore planting a life-giving church in America. The life of faith following Jesus is exciting, and it's frightening. Your purpose will not be given to you. You will discover it on the road of perseverance and persistence. The more you run your race, the more your purpose will unfold.

Suffer some, keep running some...

Finding and staying on your God-ordained path is fulfilling, but it is hardly ever easy or convenient. In fact, it can feel so difficult, painful even impossible to live out before it's fulfilling. You will even start to think the very God who

213

called you is against you because of your faults. As you stay the course running, you will look back and see that while God is working through you, He is working in you and on you, correcting and establishing things and this can only happen as we stay in the race. The amount of work God does through you will match what He is doing inside of you. God works from the inside out. That is why it is not enough to avail yourself to serve in ministry. You need to avail yourself to God. You could serve wrong, but you won't follow wrong, if you sincerely surrender to God to be your guide. Remember the Macedonian church? They gave themselves first to God and then to the ministry of serving others. Their trials, what they suffered did not distract them from keeping the main the main thing. It is easy to try and look for things to attach yourself to apart from God to ease the suffering as you run your race. Keep running back to Jesus because if you attach yourself to anything or anyone else, you will lose track and you will not learn the needed lessons and build the needed strength for what you are meant to accomplish up ahead. We build strength as we stay connected to the source.

I have fought the good fight, I have finished the race, I have kept the faith.

(2 Timothy 4:7)

The only reason Paul could say this is because he found his course, knew his track and kept it running. Paul should have very easily given up following his path considering all the beatings, the imprisonment, the suffering he experienced. In one instance that has challenged me thoroughly, Paul, at the beginning of his preaching ministry, was stoned and left for dead. When he regained consciousness, he went straight back into preaching the good news for which he had just been stoned. Many today would call him crazy in the head.

Then Jews from Antioch and Iconium came there and having persuaded the multitudes, they stoned Paul and dragged him out of the city, supposing him to be dead. However, when the disciples gathered around him, he rose up and went into the city. And the next day, he departed with Barnabas to Derbe. And when they had preached the gospel to that city and made many disciples, they returned to Lystra, Iconium, and Antioch, strengthening the souls of the disciples, exhorting them to continue in the faith, and saying, "We must through many tribulations enter the kingdom of God."

(Acts 14:19-22)

I know many church folk today who complain over some of the most trivial things. People who are inconsistent with their commitment like they were doing God a favor. They stop doing their part because it rained too much, or they couldn't find the right thing to wear or disagreed with someone at church. I have experienced some suffering as I run my race. I have been falsely accused, insulted, robbed of equipment and money. I have experienced financial hardship. I have felt sick in my body, tested for everything possible, found nothing and yet still felt sick. It is easy to think that it is God who brings about our suffering, but far from it. God does no evil. Do you remember when Job went through the trial? The perpetrator of all the suffering was Satan, not God.

God simply allowed it in order to prove Job. The sufferings you go through are proving you. They are actually a compliment, so keep running (I cannot believe I'm actually saying that, because it is never funny when you are in the midst of it all.) Even when you stumble and fall, get up and keep running.

For though a righteous man may stumble seven times, he still gets up; but the wicked stumble in bad times.

(Proverbs 24:16)

Running your race is not about being perfect. It is about being your best, receiving grace for your failures. The more grace we receive, the more strength we will have to keep running. Receive grace and drink it in abundance because, like a race car needs gas to keep going, we need grace for the race. Do you notice most of the word grace is race? The G is God and His strength.

Chapter 13

Sojourners in Transition

We were born in transition. The journey of our lives did not start when we were born. It started in God's mind. This world is not our final destiny. Some day the earth as we know it will come to an end. No one knows the day or the time, but God does, and that day is coming. But before that day comes, every human being is born, lives and then one day dies. We are sojourners on this earth and the sooner you embrace that reality, the more you will learn to live with urgency, and the less attachment you will accord this era. We tend to live like there's always tomorrow until we are reminded of the temporariness of this existence when things like the Coronavirus hit the globe or when a loved one dies. How we spend our days on earth will determine how we spend eternity. Forever is a very, very, very, very long time. In fact, it is so long. It cannot be numbered! Our days on earth are numbered, but eternity has no number. You want to be sure you are in a happy place in an endless, timeless zone. Only Jesus can bring us all to that happy place. No amount of human goodness will qualify anyone to spend eternity in Heaven. To try and get to Heaven by good works; by being a nice person is like one insisting to pay for a free gift they clearly could never afford even with all of their life's earnings put together.

And this is eternal life, that they may know You, the only true God, and Jesus Christ whom You have sent.

(John 17:3)

Eternal life is not waiting to happen someday. In this temporary human frame, there is an eternal part of us already existing. You either have Heaven in your heart or hell in your heart. I once listened to a true story of a man who experienced death on the operation table and was on his way to hell but returned to life. He described his experience as the most miserably horrendous thing he had ever felt. He said that in hell, depression is magnified, fear is magnified, sadness is magnified, despair and sorrow are magnified, hopelessness is magnified, anxiety is magnified. In other words, the life you choose now will continue into eternity, but magnified. If you have chosen the joy of the Lord, the peace that passes understanding, even in the midst of suffering in this world, if you have chosen Jesus, you will continue into eternity with those emotions magnified. Every feeling we experience in this life is an echo of our inner spiritual disposition. True peace, joy and freedom come from knowing you are so loved by God and accepting the free gift of salvation in Jesus Christ, God's only Son. If you try to save yourself by working to earn

Heaven, you insult God for the indescribable gift of Jesus hanging on a cross for the sins of mankind. Many people think that God sends people to hell because He is angry with them. No, He doesn't. Whether you end up in Heaven or hell is a matter of your choosing. God has made it that way. Like Joshua said to the children of Israel,

"Now, therefore, fear the Lord, serve Him in sincerity and in truth, and put away the gods which your fathers served on the other side of the River and in Egypt. Serve the Lord! And if it seems evil to you to serve the Lord, choose for yourselves this day whom you will serve, whether the gods which your fathers served that were on the other side of the River or the gods of the Amorites, in whose land you dwell. But as for me and my house, we will serve the Lord."

(Joshua 24:14-15)

If there is one question God will ask us on the day of judgment, I think it will go like this; ***"What did you do with my son Jesus Christ of Nazareth whom I sent to die for you on the cross?"***

God is asking that question today; What are you going to do with my son Christ Jesus of Nazareth whom I sent to die for you on the cross while you still have this life I have given you? Your life is a gift from God. What you do with it is your gift back to God or not.

It breaks God's heart when people reject Christ, the one who sacrificed His life to save humanity. When people go to hell, it's not like God is pleased saying, serves you right for rejecting me! No! God's heart breaks for humanity when people continue to reject the very path that not only brings you into eternity with Him, but also enables you to live a meaningful, purposeful life in this vapor existence. No one knows the day or the hour that God will bring about the end, but no one knows the day or the hour their own end will come either. I often take issue with people who make comments saying, Come Lord Jesus in response to the leftist so-called 'progressive' agenda that is being aggressively enforced across American universities and other parts of the world and made to look like the norm while assaulting anything that was tradition. An agenda that attacks marriage and human sexuality as God intended it. Political correctness or being nice about something in order to qualify it and make it more acceptable and less offensive, in my opinion, is misplaced, destructive 'compassion.' The truth of the Bible has never changed and will never change. Refusing to acknowledge reality in order to be less offensive, in my opinion, is like an Ostrich in the jungles of Africa putting its head in the sand and thinking that because it cannot see its pursuer, the pursuer is not there. That Ostrich always becomes an easy meal for the lions and Hyenas.

We followers of Jesus are meant to respond to an agenda that goes against Christ with a Kingdom agenda. What we cry out for God to do something about, He oftentimes expects us to challenge and stand up to with the truth. While we say Come Lord Jesus, Jesus is up in Heaven saying, before I return, what are you doing about it? You see, many of us might not see the return of the Lord Jesus in our lifetime. We might already be gone and have met Him by then. In the meantime, He is asking us; What are you going to do for the Kingdom while you are alive? You are a sojourner. What will you accomplish and leave as a legacy for your time on earth?

What are you going to do for your generation before the curtain closes on you? I want to hear God say well done, good and faithful servant to me when the curtain closes on my existence in this form. I hope you do too.

When my mum had a stroke and my earthly father died within two weeks of each other, God said to me; This life is short son. What are you going to do with it while you still have it?

That statement sobered me up! God knows how to get you out of your pity party and help you to see things clearly. The people you spend your days mourning about don't actually care. Not because they do not, but they are dead da! They cannot feel a thing. If they are in Heaven, if they chose Jesus as their Savior, they are rejoicing and dancing their hearts away in everlasting bliss in the presence of Jesus and here you are, crying over them. They would rather you went on about living your life to the best of your ability because someday your end will come too and you will join them. If they rejected Jesus and are in hell, they are hoping you do not end up there, like in the story of Lazarus and the rich man.

"There was a rich man who was dressed in purple and fine linen and lived in luxury every day. At his gate was laid a beggar named Lazarus, covered with sores and longing to eat what fell from the rich man's table. Even the dogs came and licked his sores. The time came when the beggar died and the angels carried him to Abraham's side. The rich man also died and was buried. In Hades, where he was in torment, he looked up and saw Abraham far away, with Lazarus by his side. So he called to him, 'Father Abraham, have pity on me and send Lazarus to dip the tip of his finger in water and cool my tongue, because I am in agony in this fire.' "But Abraham replied,

'Son, remember that in your lifetime you received your good things, while Lazarus received bad things, but now he is comforted here and you are in agony. And besides all this, between you and us a great chasm has been set in place, so that those who want to go from here to you cannot, nor can anyone cross over from there to us.' "He answered, 'Then I beg you, father, send Lazarus to my family, for I have five brothers. Let him warn them, so that they will not also come to this place of torment.' "Abraham replied, 'They have Moses and the Prophets; let them listen to them.' "'No, father Abraham,' he said, 'but if someone from the dead goes to them, they will repent.' "He said to him, 'If they do not listen to Moses and the Prophets, they will not be convinced even if someone rises from the dead.'"

(Luke 16:19-31)

Both my parents are in Heaven because they chose Jesus as their Lord and Savior. I miss them sometimes, but I look at God's working in their lives and how they got to know Him and I am grateful I will see them again in Heaven. Do not wait for something drastic to happen before you make the most important decision of your life to give yourself completely to Jesus.

Now I do not want in any way to downplay the importance of relationships with departed loved ones. But one thing I want to say is, sometimes we use grieving for a long time to cover up an underlying issue of depression or bitterness or anger or other issues we have never really addressed, which we sometimes cover up by 'over mourning' when we lose a loved one.

The grief reveals what has been an underlying issue. I know this because God challenged me on my depression and bitterness and holding on to issues and the victim mentality when I was dealing with the death of my earthly father and my mum having a stroke in a space of two weeks. A victim mentality is always looking for a reason to blame or something to mourn about. Sometimes people with issues may appear like the most grieved with their tears in a given loss, but that is just their inside issues in play. I want to share with you some of the things that transpired when my mother had a stroke.

You see, I consider myself a man of faith. I believe that God can do anything. In fact, I graduated from just believing to knowing that God can do anything. Do I still have questions? Yes, indeed I do! I often get so confused about life because even though I completely believe God, sometimes I have to wait for a long time to see the fruit of my faith. Sometimes it feels like it's never happening, and I am wasting my time or God's time or there's something wrong with my faith.

I went over to my mum's house when she had the stroke with the determination to see her healed. I prayed over her, anointed her with oil, I even tried to get her upright on her feet to walk by faith. It looked like it was working for a little while, but she stumbled right back down. Did I give up? No, I kept believing and praying, but my mother, even though she recovered a little, did not come back to normal.

Now God has healed me before from a persistent headache, from high blood pressure, common colds and flus and other things I don't even know. I have felt His physical touch! I have prayed for people and they have been healed. So I asked God why not my mum? I cried out to Him, but nothing happened. God will sometimes answer us as we ask, other times not as we ask, but He will always give the appropriate answer. Sometimes God answers by redirecting our focus. Sometimes God wants to teach us to accept the inevitability and the frailty of this life as it is. Teach us to embrace life in all its forms while holding on to the eternal. My mother's time was almost up and I needed to accept that and try to make the best of my own time. Was that easy to accept? No!

There is a time for everything and a season for every activity under the heavens: a time to be born and a time to die, a time to plant and a time to uproot.

(Ecclesiastes 3:1-2)

My mother only recovered a little from the stroke and stayed alive for two years recovering before she passed on. I was over the whole mourning thing by that time. By then, we had started the church and it was growing. I went and led the church in song and preached a sermon, then announced at the end of the service that my mother had passed away and we were going to have a funeral the next day. The people at church were shocked that I still came in and did what I did like nothing had happened. You should know that I loved my mother very much. She was my most loyal human. She had suffered as a parent dealing with my instability as a teenager growing up but did not give up on me. When I got a job and blessings started flowing my way, I wanted to bless my mother. I built her a house, bought her what she needed. I would have done anything for my mother, except could not heal her. Some things will help you accept that you can only do so much for the people you love. I know my mother is in Heaven because she loved Jesus.

When my mother died, I saw in a dream the previous night that she was entering a boat-like caravan in a clear blue sky. Later that day, I received the news that she had passed on. I loved my mother, felt the pain of her passing, I grieved my mother, God knows how much that affected me and continued to affect me, but I have gone on about my business because one day it will be me and I hope to have done everything I'm supposed to do in this realm before I transfer into eternity. Do not hold on to your departed loved ones so much that it hinders you from living the life they would want you to live. God is constantly challenging me about attachments. He would rather that we hold on with a tight grip to that which we cannot lose and hold on with a thin grip to that which is temporal. Many people suffer much anxiety and fear in this life because they have these two things interchanged.

Treasure you cannot lose!

But lay up for yourselves treasures in heaven, where neither moth nor rust destroys and where thieves do not break in and steal. For where your treasure is, there your heart will be also.

(Matthew 6:20-21)

Every time God asks us to take a risk, a step of faith, He is winning us from the predictable to the unpredictable. He is winning us of earthly attachments and to Himself. God is winning us from the temporal to the eternal. When I started to trust God in faith, at first, I did not understand why things had to be so complicated. Why don't we just get from A to B?

PETER J. WAMONO

I mean, do you not trust me, God? When God calls us to something, He calls us to Himself first. God wants to know if He is enough for you. Some people make serving God more important than following Him closely. You will end up doing your own thing and all you will hear in the end is away from me. I never knew you. Following Jesus is not a straight road. He will bring you on to detours, dead-end roads, potholes and bumps. There will be some straight roads too, but mostly winding, hilly roads. The journey will take you through valleys and over mountain tops, but every avenue will have meaning for you. God said this to me once; *"What seem like dead ends are your conversations with me that you have not yet understood."*

Now the Lord had said to Abram: "Get out of your country, From your family and from your father's house, to a land that I will show you. I will make you a great nation; I will bless you and make your name great; and you shall be a blessing. I will bless those who bless you, and I will curse him who curses you; And in you all the families of the earth shall be blessed."

(Genesis 12:1-3)

Before God does amazing things in our lives and make no mistake, He does want us to give Him a chance to let Him do astronomical things through us. He will ask us to lose attachments. You see, God wants to know that when He opens the Heavens and entrusts you with Heaven's purpose, you will not use your influence to go after earthly things and fulfill earthly desires. I have dreamed of building some amazing buildings for our church campuses in Uganda, 5000 to 7000 seat auditoriums. I know we will build them one day. I have also dreamed of building an airport for the town where we are so I can fly in and preach in the most happening place Sunday morning and fly out and preach in Miami, Florida, Sunday evening the same day. I'm crazy, right! I think God can do anything. I have always said this to my team and church and I believe it's true.

"When God knows that He means more to you than anything in this world, He will entrust you with earthly blessings because He knows they will not take His place in your life. He knows that you will use what He entrusts you with as a means to an eternal end, to serve the purposes of the Kingdom."

You might say I have been faithful to God, but He has not entrusted me yet, something wrong with me? Absolutely not! God has a timing, a rhythm and He knows your rhythm. Your time will come. Just keep being faithful where you are with what you have. Keep forgetting the past and its pain and hurt. Serving your purpose and running your race requires a whole lot of patience and perseverance and tenacity.

The fruit of the righteous is a tree of life, And he who wins souls is wise.

(Proverbs 11:30)

Chapter 14

A People Under God

I shared in a previous chapter that I have been to most parts of the United States of America. People often ask me what state or city I like the most, and if you are asking too, I won't really say. I mean, it's not like I fell in love with Hawaii or something. Let me tell you what caught my attention the first time I came to America. First of all, it was that song, *"America the Beautiful!"*

We got to sing that song on our Watoto choir tours at many churches across many states and I witnessed the impact the chorus had on people.

*"America, America, God shed His grace on thee
And crown thy good with brotherhood
From sea to shining sea..."*

There were tears in the eyes of people across the entire audience everywhere we sung it. This song got people, and it got me. Another thing that got me was *"One nation under God."*

I don't mean to boast, but ever since I came into a relationship with Jesus Christ and brought my life under God, my life has been on an upward tangent. It's not like there have not been hard days. There have been many, as you have read in my story. But, my life under God has been like one who hit the jackpot, who won the Powerball lottery, won the prettiest girl in school. I actually did that in high school, but that's not the point here.

It breaks my heart that some people downplay the value of the statement, **"One Nation Under God"** in America, and even want to strip it from being part of the pledge of allegiance as I have seen some leaders in the Democrat party do. There is but one God - Yahweh, and to be under God means everything for America. To identify with God is like identifying with the most powerful man on earth and having Him in your inner circle as your buddy. Who doesn't want that? Only a fool. A nation under God means everything for any nation in the world. No country is perfect, no people are perfect, every nation and culture has a history, but it is the things that shape a society into something beautiful that we ought to celebrate even as we try to avoid repeating evil history. I have been to most parts of the world like I shared earlier and I have not felt the atmosphere of freedom and opportunity anywhere like I have felt here in America. Many people outside America do not want to come to America for nothing. It is the God factor of freedom - "Liberty and justice for all." "The land of the free and the home of the brave." Make no mistake of this, the day America ceases to be a nation under God, the land of the free and home of the brave with liberty and justice for all, which are all God factors, is the day people outside America will cease to desire to come out here. It will become like any other nation and why would anyone want to come to something that is no different from where they already are.

A legacy of a nation under God is worth holding on to with dear life. Some will say that it means nothing because of the evil history of racism in America, but I beg to defer. I have been to black history museums in Jackson, Mississippi, Birmingham, Alabama and Nashville, Tennessee specifically and purposefully in order to research and understand the complex history of the United States of America as it pertains to race issues. I do not like to take what I hear in the media without researching it for myself. I do not want to make light of racism because I have seen its evil effect on people, plus I have experienced a little bit of it myself because of my skin color and background. Racism is evil, but so is stealing and murder, and lying and all the things that violate, disenfranchise and hurt others. Even though much of the racism has often been a black and white issue, it is also a Latino and Asian and Indian issue. It is a tribal issue in Africa and other parts of the world. It is a human heart issue. Black people can be prejudiced against other black people, just like white people can be about other white people and so on and so forth.

Just because America has a history of racism does not mean America cannot truly be a nation under God. What if everything you stand for today that is positive in your life was dismissed as nothing because of all the negative things you stood for in your past or the mistakes you are making today? Would that be fair? I do not think so. Aren't people allowed to change? I think that there will always be room for improvement in this human frame, room to right wrongs, but involving God in a broken society is the glue that holds a society together and shines a light in the darkness showing the way up. Without God, there is no true justice. The only way is down.

True justice

I once visited an aboriginal village in Australia and noticed there were a lot of broken-down cars on the side of the road. I asked someone in the community we visited why this was. They said to me that Aboriginal people receive cars from the Australian government but do not service them. They drive them until they drop them. They only return to the dead car for spare parts for the next car they get or to sell for money. Some of the cars have not even covered more than 15,000 miles. Apparently, the Australian government has a financial reparation system in place for what the Aboriginals suffered under white immigrant settlers in Australia. They give them free cars and money, plus mandated discounts at places of business. I noticed a lot of Aboriginal people sitting under trees in the middle of the day in Alice Springs, a town in the outback of Australia under the influence of alcohol who spent their days drinking their lives away using the free money they receive and I thought to myself, how is this helping these people fulfill their purpose except to waste their lives away?

I think that if something has been stolen, there should be payback where possible. But paying out handouts to people because of past evils as a remorse offering never empowers the individual. It only acts as a disincentive for creativity and personal responsibility. Racism is evil, but handouts are undignified. We must not use evil as an excuse to perpetuate negativity, to get a free pass in life or escape personal responsibility. I do not want to make light of racism. I absolutely abhor it. But here's what I'm saying. Everyone suffers evil at one point or another, and many people have misrepresented God in the name of religion, but that has never been an excuse to denounce "One nation under God."

God was there when Egypt enslaved Israel for 400 years. He brought deliverance to the nation of Israel and gave them a nation. Today Israel stands as an independent nation manufacturing things and creating technology that is changing the world, making their mark on the world, but they did not have it easy even after 400 years in slavery. They have worked hard, fought for their inheritance to become the nation they are today. The evils in the world are evidence there is a bad devil. But there is a good God, and more of God than a created, fallen angel, that's why there is so much more good in the world than there is evil, and blessed is the nation whose God is the Lord. God alone knows how to make things right, how to bring about the rightful recompense where there has been injustice. Democracy can only bring about a cosmetic fix to racism or any kind of evil. It has no power to fix the hearts of men. The root of evil can only be uprooted when people are truly under the God of all creation and the Lordship of Jesus Christ, His only Son, not religion. There is but one God who changes the hearts of men. All else is behavior modification that has no lasting impact.

I grew up in Uganda, a nation that was founded not under God, but under animism. Our ancestors believed in superstition, in trees, rocks, mountains, lakes, rivers until European missionaries arrived with the 'good news' of the Catholic Church and Anglican Church. Before that, the Muslim faith had made its way in, but did not gain traction like the Catholic and Anglican faiths did. The latter gained traction because, along with their message, they built schools and churches and hospitals. Some of our ancestors embraced Christianity in Catholicism and Anglicanism, some even died for their newfound faith, but most practiced these faiths as a part of what they already had, not as the WAY. They did not abandon their old animistic beliefs but added going to church to that. One would go to church on Sunday and then to the witch doctor on Tuesday. There are people still doing this today. You could be as contemporary as possible in your faith, but the Bible says manipulation of any kind is as witchcraft. Manipulation and control lingers where there is no faith in God.

Religion in itself has no power to change people or transform nations. It is the person of Jesus Christ who is the game-changer. Christianity must be embraced wholly as the way, not as an alternative to something else or it will be impotent to bring about transformation among a people.

At independence from the British in 1962, Uganda's leaders were in consultation with the occult. They dedicated the nation to idol gods by performing rituals acknowledging spirits. Now there are those who reason that every path leads to God, but that is a lie from the pit of hell. There is but one path to God and there is but one God and the way to Him is through Jesus Christ, His only Son, who is the prince of peace. This is not my opinion. It is simply the truth everyone alive today will have to contend with when their time comes and they meet their maker. Uganda has suffered decades of chaos and turmoil and only started to enjoy peace with the rising of the church of Jesus Christ.

The game-changer!

Jesus is the game-changer for nations. Everywhere He is acknowledged, transformation happens, lives are made beautiful. I want to tell you a story about northern Uganda to help you understand the importance of what I'm saying about being a nation under God.

You may or may not have heard about Joseph Kony. He was a rebel leader who terrorized the northern part of Uganda for decades. He killed hundreds of thousands and abducted thousands of boys and girls, turning them into child soldiers and forcing little girls to become soldier wives. Young girls 10, 11 and12 years old became wives and had children. Many died in the process. Their lives were considered worthless. Young boys were forced to shoot and kill their own families as part of a rebel initiation process to turn them into merciless killing machines. It was evil. Joseph Kony operated under the influence of the occult, under spiritual demonic powers of witchcraft, the same powers our nation of Uganda was brought under at independence in 1962.

For decades, the Uganda government army tried to get rid of the rebel army, but the rebels always eluded them. In a video which you can watch for free on YouTube called "The Unconventional war," one of the rebel commanders says that the rebel army eluded the Uganda government army by the power of witchcraft. People in the church started to have dreams and visions in which the government was losing the war against the rebels, but pastors and Christian leaders were fighting and defeating them. A member of my Wednesday fellowship had a dream and shared in which Uganda's president was being defeated by the rebel leader in a boxing match, but when he stood up and said I defeat you, Joseph Kony in the name of Jesus, the rebel leader was vanquished.

The church mobilized in prayer and fasting to address the rebel activity on the spiritual level on which they were operating. Pastors and church leaders, in conjunction with the Uganda government, went to the northern part of the country and exhumed human skeletons while destroying witchcraft alters where human sacrifices had been made. As prayers went up and alters were destroyed, Joseph Kony started to lose his grip and the government gained an upper hand over the rebel army that had eluded them for decades and drove them out of Uganda. As I write this, the northern part of Uganda has been peaceful for over 16 years. There are beautiful National parks with lions, elephants and other wildlife that my business takes people to marvel at. These parks were inaccessible for a long time because of the rebel activity in the northern part of the country. Also, in some of the land, the rebels used as a base to terrorize and abduct and kill thousands. Watoto, the organization I worked with, has built a children's village that is helping former child soldiers become future leaders of their community and nation. Many people ask me if it's safe in Uganda and I say to them not in the past, but much of Uganda today is safer than parts of Chicago or New York. Coming from Uganda, looking at my history, I can understand and appreciate the value of being a nation under God. We desire it, we yearn for it, we want it because we know that there is but one God; Yahweh, Elohim and if it were not for God, the children who now have a home and are growing to become leaders in their nation would still be caught up in a destructive cycle of witchcraft and occultism. Uganda still has a very long way to go in fulfilling its true destiny as a nation, but one thing is for sure; We know that to be a nation under God is a game-changer for any community and nation. It is something to look up to, not to shun, mock, make light of and look down on.

> For even if there are so-called gods, whether in heaven or on earth (as there are many gods and many lords), yet for us, there is one God, the Father, of whom are all things, and we for Him; and one Lord Jesus Christ, through whom are all things, and through whom we live.

(1 Corinthians 8:5-6)

If you observe carefully, nations around the world with chaotic regimes and massive corruption are nations that are under the influence of witchcraft and idolatry. Countries and their citizens suffer more and more corruption the more distant they are from the God of all creation. The God factor in a nation is the moral authority, the spirit that causes restraint and sets the spiritual atmosphere and influences ways of life of societies and nations. What we now call western society evolved out of the influence of the God factor. Witches, savages and barbarians in ancient Europe were transformed by the good news of Jesus Christ that led to the era of enlightenment that caused an industrial revolution that created the western lifestyle. The God factor was the game changer! The people who moved to America as pilgrims out of Europe in the early 1600's sought to create a society where they had free, uncontrolled practice of their faith. They did not want someone telling them how to relate to God. They were not perfect people, but they had it right. At the core of the Christian faith is love and freedom!

Even with the fake news seeking to determine what is considered as truth and what is not, plus all the anti-Christ agenda's currently in play in America, God has a remnant and a plan. As long as one nation under God is still in play, there will be restraint because the spirit of God Himself is at work. The day that America completely abandons God and removes Him from everything is the day the restraint will be removed and anything will go. There will be no standard and America as the world has known it will cease to be. I know this is already in play; the so-called "progressive" redefining of America like removing prayer in schools is an assault on America that has been in play for the last 60 years and has led to moral decline and a rise in criminal activity. Most cities in America that adhere to so-called progressive leadership, also suffer the most from homelessness, gangs, criminal activity and drugs. Los Angeles, San Francisco, Baltimore, Chicago, New York City, to name but a few, are all under progressive leadership and are reported to have the highest crime rates and highest homelessness in America. The progressive agenda is not that progressive after all, is it? You can change the name of criminal activity and homelessness to sound less offensive and more "progressive," but it still what it is. A well-dressed and decorated pig is still a pig and will act like one. The Bible says.

Jesus Christ is the same yesterday and today and forever.

(Hebrews 13:8)

Everything Jesus said thousands of years ago still means the same today. Everything the Bible says from the time it was written thousands of years ago has not changed in meaning or purpose. The way the gospel is preached has evolved, but the gospel message itself has not 'progressed' one bit and will never change.

A people that once had God and abandoned God become a lost people and lose their identity and their place of influence on the world.

God + identity!

I consider myself a deep person, I tend to look at things beyond the surface, so I hate small talk. I like to have deep, meaningful conversations. When something impacts me, it stays. I have learned and keep learning that I should not brush off things that impact me deeply because God uses those things to communicate His purposes. If you have been reading this book from the start, you must be thinking, just how deep is this guy really lol? I shared how the embarrassment and shame I associated with my earthly father's alcoholism affected my acceptance of self. It made me a pretender who always preferred a false identity to escape my reality. It also made me a very shallow individual, even though I thought I was deep.

I have learned how the enemy undermines men and women in this world. He wants to shame you to shallowness, so you live your life average without passion, without standing up for anything because of fear. Without passion, there cannot be a real impact in life. You are simply existing. The devil likes that because he knows you won't be a threat to the kingdom of darkness that way. When you hide your true self, you build a shell around you that makes you a 'shell' of an individual (Hahaha......get it!).

God knows how to take us into the shallowness of our shell and break into the beautiful underlying depth He placed inside of us. The more broken we are, the more effective we can be because our true light emerges out of our broken shell.

God and I know the journey we have been on together. I must say I have always known I was a deep person. But I also allowed keeping up appearances to keep me shallow. This caused me to fail in a lot of potentially wonderful relationships. Girls have fallen in love with the surface level me that was bubbly and seemed happy and sort of deep, but the truth is I was just a shell of a guy. Okay, I'll stop using that line, I promise. Can't even believe I use that on myself. Like Rafiki in the Lion King says, "It's in dee past! You can run from it, or you can learn from it!"

Sometimes I have run away from potentially good relationships because I knew I was shallow and did not want to face it, for a girl to find me out hahaha. Honestly, I have harbored this fear that I may appear impressive to people with my friendly, welcoming personality, but scared I may not live up to my original impression. I might ruin it. I know you do not identify, but that's me and God has been working on me, with me, giving me a new identity and I'm daily discovering who I am, A child of God and want to live from that place of power and freedom continually.

Knowing who you are in God shapes who you become to society. Those who do not know God also do not really know who they are. Everything about who we are and are meant to be in this life starts with God and in God. When God is removed from our lives and society, it's not just God who leaves. Identity leaves, purpose leaves, meaning leaves, people are lost and they do not know why. People do not become criminals because they love it. It is because they are looking for an identity. If you will go back with me and look at America over the last 60 years. The level of drugs and crimes, including murder rates, have grown increasingly with departing from prayer in schools and the things of God becoming offensive. In fact, school communities started losing their true and meaningful impact on the nation when praying to the God of all creation became an offense. When everything else is allowed but the God of all creation, nothing has meaning. We are like a bunch of people sitting in rocking chairs, hoping to get somewhere far. Our identity as humans is tied to and found in the God of all creation - Yahweh, and without God, there is never-ending chaos. God brings sanity to society.

When 911 happened back in 2001, Billy Graham very much alive then was asked this question. Where was God when this happened? Why did He not protect us? Billy Graham responded, "God was right where you left Him, out of your lives."

Time and time again, God left the children of Israel to their own devices, and the enemy overrun them. Why? Because they abandoned God and turned to worship of idols who could not protect or save them, they chose their own way. Idolatry is anything you have valued more than God. It could be a job, money, a lifestyle, an addiction, someone you are obsessed with etc. But when Israel cried out to God again, He always came to their defense again like nothing happened. God is good like that. He does not hold a grudge. God does not force His way with men either. He will only show up and show out where He is invited. God gave men free will. As one preacher said, *"The greatest risk God took on humanity was not to send Jesus, but to give men free will."*

"But if you or your descendants abandon me and disobey the commands and decrees I have given you, and if you serve and worship other gods, then I will uproot Israel from this land that I have given them. I will reject this Temple that I have made holy to honor my name. I will make Israel an object of mockery and ridicule among the nations. And though this Temple is impressive now, all who pass by will be appalled and will gasp in horror. They will ask, 'Why did the Lord do such terrible things to this

land and to this Temple?' "And the answer will be, 'Because his people abandoned the Lord their God, who brought their ancestors out of Egypt, and they worshiped other gods instead and bowed down to them. That is why the Lord has brought all these disasters on them.'"

(1 Kings 9:6-9)

I want to share with you some of the things God has personally spoken to me concerning America. On one of my trips across America back in October 2018, I was in the city of Dallas, Texas, alone in my room when I heard an audible voice whisper, ***"God has a plan to save America from going down the slippery slope of self-destruction."***

I thought someone was under the bed. But this voice was speaking from inside me. God was speaking to me about a people He still so loves. A few days later, I heard another whisper from God concerning America: ***"silent Jihad."***

If you do not know what a Jihad is, it is a struggle to advance the cause of Islam with whatever means necessary, including forceful means.

When you abandon your heritage under God, mock it, make light of it, you make room for anything that goes to become your new way of life. A nation under God that abandons God makes room for everything else while sidelining the God who alone is responsible for creating an environment of freedom and peace. When the God of freedom leaves, so does His freedom along with Him. You cannot want what God has while sidelining His involvement in your life.

God loves all the nations and all the people of the world and is waiting to be invited to take precedence over our lives in order to allow His Kingdom to rule on earth. This is the mandate of the church; To establish the Kingdom of Heaven on earth.

I beg to defer with many people I have heard say there is an impending judgment on America and America's best days are over. The truth is People and societies suffer the consequences of bad choices, and judgment day will certainly come for all of humanity, but God has not given up on America. He is patiently waiting for His church to rise up and bring about an awakening and a harvest. There is a remnant. Before God brings judgment, He always offers grace. He calls people to repentance. We dare not resign, saying, come Lord Jesus! The people in the Bible that Paul talks about in the book of Romans thought the end was near when apostasy and evil were rife, but millenniums later, we are still here to read their story. We ought to stand up so that many years from now, generations to come will read about our generation as those who stood up and served their Kingdom purpose and allowed God's revival plan to unfold on nations. God has a plan and that plan will unfold in concert with His church. We, the church, are God's correction and implementation officers to establish Heaven's will on earth. The harvest is plentiful, but the harvesters are few. I'm glad He chose me to be part of His plan for humanity. This is my mission in Uganda, America and the ends of the earth.

And this gospel of the kingdom will be preached in the whole world as a testimony to all nations, and then the end will come.

(Matthew 24:14)

While we are awaiting our Savior's return, we have to find our stations and man them. We have to love the world like Jesus does, not the way the world wants to be loved. The love of Jesus challenges us, changes us and brings out the best in us, tells us the truth even when it hurts. Jesus will accept you as you are, but He will never leave you as you are.

Love does not delight in evil but rejoices with the truth.

(1 Corinthians 13:7)

I have always prayed to God for as long as I remember and as long as I have been on this journey of discovering my own identity that my life would be poured out as an offering. That God would use me anyhow, in any way and anywhere. I made myself available to God. It is a decision that gets tested every day and whose depth of meaning I keep grasping every day. It is uncomfortable and inconvenient, sometimes painful, there is suffering involved, but I could not trade it for anything else in the whole wide world.

Living your life with an eternal focus under God will help you travel light. It will also help you process the disappointing and heartbreaking things you experience in this vapor time better. An eternal focus will bring definition and purpose to your life like nothing ever can. The greatest legacy a man/woman can leave to their children is not money or property but a life under God. Everything is temporary. But a legacy under God. No one can steal that. It is what will enable your benefactors and make good of the money and property you leave behind.

> *Blessed are those who dwell in your house; they are ever praising you. Blessed are those whose strength is in you, whose hearts are set on pilgrimage.*

(Psalms 84:4-5)

I want us to stop and pray the prayer Jesus taught us to pray.

> *Our Father in heaven, may your name be kept holy. May your Kingdom come soon. May your will be done on earth, as it is in heaven. Give us today the food we need, and forgive us our sins, as we have forgiven those who sin against us. And don't let us yield to temptation, but rescue us from the evil one. Yours is the Kingdom, the power and glory. Forever and ever and ever and ever and ever.......Amen*

(Matthew 6:9-13)

Conclusion

I do not know where you are in your journey following Jesus. What I do know is you may be at the start, the honeymoon stage, excited and thankful for this unconditional love you just experienced. Rejoice; you just made the best decision of your life. Like Billy Graham said, *"I have never seen someone give their hearts to Jesus and regret it later."*

Following Jesus is the best decision anyone can make. It will most certainly get challenging as you go along, but every challenge will be cut to the continuity of your journey, to the person you are called to be if you stay standing through the challenges.

You may be a few years in and confused, feeling overwhelmed with questions. Well, questions are healthy for a Christ-follower, because there are a lot of things in the spiritual world we will not understand in the moment. We only comprehend them in hindsight. To not have questions is to assume that you know. The truth is, we are all just discovering what this life of following and serving a spiritual, supernatural and perfect God in our natural, mortal, broken flesh is like. If you have questions, take them all to Jesus. And if you still do not understand, SURRENDER! He knows so much better than we do.

I hope my story gave you some insight, but ultimately, the Holy Spirit is with you and is able to give you an understanding of perplexing things, plus comfort you and give you peace in confusion.

I have learned we often miss out on a beautiful and deep peace because we do not bring our questions to the right place. I know this will sound so shallow, but when in a classroom attending a lesson and you do not understand a particular part of a subject, you ask the teacher to explain, right? The teacher feels valuable and needed when you ask those questions and they are able to give explanations. Well, the Holy Spirit feels the same when we take our questions to Him. He is our teacher. The Bible says, *"He will lead us into all truth." (John 16:13)*

The questions are nothing but invitations to a deeper conversation and fellowship with God. The place of confusion is also a place of spiritual enlightenment. The enemy will try to lie to us in moments of confusion, painting his own deceptive picture of who God is for us to believe. Do not wrestle or argue with the enemy. The best way to fight the enemy is by speaking the truth of God like Jesus did; It is written.

I wish I were an expert at this, still learning to stand in the truth myself. Still growing, but I have come a long, long way. When we bring our confusion to Jesus, we find peace, and that is our place of power in the world.

I will finish with this; Your IDENTITY and mine are tied to knowing Jesus and knowing that we are known by Him. Every experience God calls us into will reveal more of that identity. To say no to God, to disobey His instructions (and they can be uncomfortable and inconvenient, as I have shared), is to deny yourself the opportunity of discovering who you really are.

Thank you for taking this journey with me. I hope this book has been a blessing to you. I will be following this book up with my next one, 'STABILITY', which will be another candid tale of this unstable soul learning to stand on a firm foundation of divine love in a shaky world. If you would like to reach out to me with a question or feedback, please send me an email: peter@musaalechurch.com

God bless you!

Peter

Made in the USA
Columbia, SC
25 September 2021